Word® for Windows First Run

Dan Speers

que COLLEGE

Word for Windows First Run

Copyright © 1993 by Que® Corporation.

Library of Congress Catalog No.: 93-85778

ISBN: 1-56529-427-0

96 95 94 93   4 3 2 1

Interpretation of the printing code: the rightmost double-digit number is the year of the book's printing; the rightmost single-digit number, the number of the book's printing. For example, a printing code of 93-1 shows that the first printing of the book occurred in 1993.

Screens reproduced in this book were created using Collage Plus from Inner Media, Inc., Hollis, NH.

Word for Windows First Run is based on Word for Windows 2.0.

Publisher: David P. Ewing

Associate Publisher: Rick Ranucci

Publishing Plan Manager: Thomas A. Bennett

Book Designer: Amy Peppler-Adams

Production Team: Angela Bannan, Danielle Bird, Paula Carroll, Laurie Casey, Charlotte Clapp, Brook Farling, Michael Hughes, Bob LaRoche, Joy Dean Lee, Jay Lesandrini, Beth Rago, Lillian Yates

Editorial Director
Carol Crowell

Series Editor
M.T. Cozzola Cagnina

Managing Editor
Sheila Cunningham

Editorial Coordinator
Elizabeth D. Brown

Formatter
Jill Stanley

Composed in *Garamond* and *MCPdigital* by Que Corporation

About the Author

Dan Speers is a corporate consultant and trainer with an extensive background in computer programming. He specializes in developing interactive tutorials, multimedia sales and training systems, and activity-based courseware. His software and educational materials have been widely used by both universities and Fortune 500 companies.

Acknowledgments

Que College is grateful for the assistance provided by the following reviewers: Jean S. Insinga, Middlesex Community College; Michael Jeffries of the University of Tampa; and Nancy Sallee of Lexington Community College. A special thanks also to our technical editor, Lynda Michelle Reader of the College of DuPage.

Trademarks

All terms mentioned in this book that are known to be trademarks or service marks have been appropriately capitalized. Que cannot attest to the accuracy of this information. Use of a term in this book should not be regarded as affecting the validity of any trademark or service mark.

Table of Contents

Preface 1

1 The Opening Window 3

2 Writing 13

3 Retrieving and Revising a Document 25

4 Using Editing Tools 35

Testing Your Skills 1 44

5 Accenting Characters 47

6 Shaping Paragraphs 54

7 Designing Pages 65

Testing Your Skills 2 75

8 Working with Files 79

9 Working in Styles 88

10 Featuring Templates 96

Testing Your Skills 3 103

Glossary 105

Index 111

Preface

The *First Run* series is designed for the novice computer user who wants to learn the basics of a software application as quickly as possible.

First Run combines practical explanations of new concepts and hands-on steps and exercises to build proficiency quickly. Each *First Run* is organized into an average of ten Teaching Units. Each Teaching Unit teaches an important skill set. The objectives that make up each Teaching Unit build on one another, section by section. Within each section are steps for performing the function or using the feature, plus an exercise to build your skills. Definitions of new terms and notes on working more effectively also are included.

First Run also offers Testing Your Skills sections to enable an instructor to evaluate progress. A glossary of terms is included in every book.

Each section in a unit takes an average of 15 minutes to complete. Since each exercise is tied directly to the current section, instructors can instantly determine a student's progress before continuing to the next section.

An **Instructor's Resource Disk** is available upon adoption of the textbook. It contains answers to all of the exercises in the textbook, as well as suggested lecture notes, additional teaching tips and information, extra optional exercises, completed data files, and other data files used in the course.

The unique combination of features in this concise guide makes *First Run* an ideal textbook for step-by-step teaching now and for easy reference later on. Instructors may mix and match individual textbooks in order to design a custom software applications course.

Look for the following additional titles in the First Run series:

WordPerfect 5.1 First Run	1-56529-428-9
WordPerfect 6 First Run	1-56529-429-7
Windows 3.1 First Run	1-56529-425-4
Excel for Windows First Run	1-56529-420-3
Basic First Run	1-56529-416-5
MS.DOS First Run	1-56529-423-8
Lotus 1-2-3 First Run (covers 2.4 and below)	1-56529-421-1
Introduction to PCs First Run	1-56529-417-3
Novell Netware First Run	1-56529-424-6
WordPerfect for Windows	1-56529-430-0
dBASE III Plus First Run	1-56529-418-1
dBASE IV First Run	1-56529-419-X

For more information call:
1-800-428-5331
or contact your local Prentice Hall College Representative.

The Opening Window

1

Starting the Word for Windows program from within the Windows *environment* (the various screens, menus, icons, and commands that make up the Windows operating system or a Windows program) is easy. If you are not already in the Windows environment, type **win** at the command prompt and press ⏎Enter.

1. Open the Windows group that contains the icon for Microsoft Word.

2. Double-click the Microsoft Word icon.

The first thing you will see when Word for Windows starts is the opening screen which operates in the Windows environment. This means that many of the menus, commands, functions, dialog boxes, and icons you use with Windows are similar to those you use in Word for Windows.

Everything you do in Word for Windows begins with this screen. This is where you create and edit your documents. This is where you select the menu options and tools you will use to enhance, save, and print your documents. This is where you can create the templates, macros, and other functions to be described later in this text that allow you to automatically repeat certain tasks and automate tedious activities.

Objectives

1.1 To Understand the Screen

1.2 To Choose Menus

1.3 To Use Dialog Boxes

1.4 To Get Help

1.1 To Understand the Screen

Compare the opening Word for Windows screen in Fig. 1.1 with the screen that now appears on your computer and examine the various parts.

Fig. 1.1
The opening screen
for Word for Windows.

Title Bar Displays the program name and the name of the document in which you are working.

Control-menu Box for Word Includes commands for changing the size of the application screen, closing the current session, switching to other programs, and running other commands.

Control-Menu Box for Document Allows you to switch to the next open document, to split the screen, or to change the size of the document window.

Ribbon Makes selected text boldface, underlined, or italic; controls paragraph alignment; and customizes tab settings.

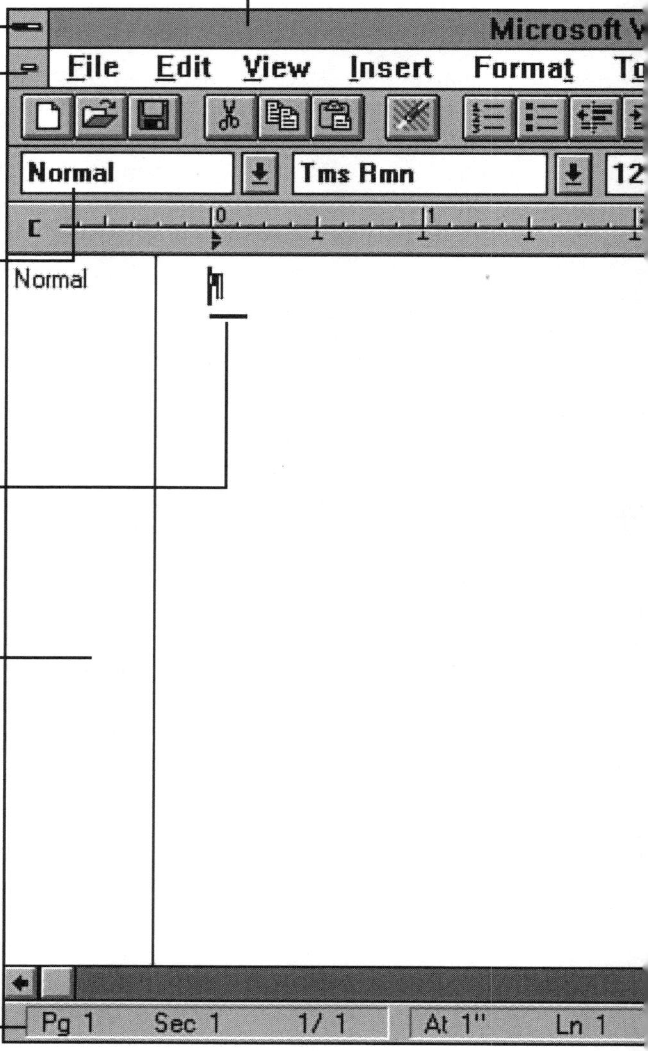

Insertion Point A horizontal bar marks the end of the document and a flashing vertical bar indicates where text will appear when you begin to type.

Style Area Word for Windows assigns a style. In the Style Area you can see the name of the style for each paragraph. The Style area appears only if you choose it as one of your options.

Status Bar Displays pertinent information about the page that contains the insertion point or about the highlighted command.

4

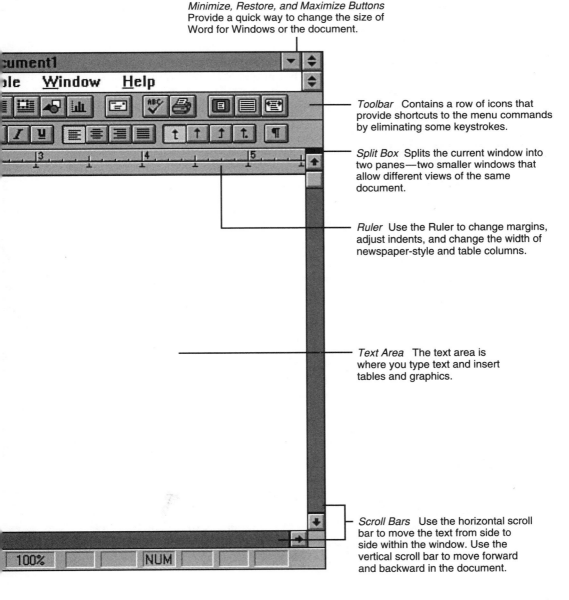

Minimize, Restore, and Maximize Buttons
Provide a quick way to change the size of
Word for Windows or the document.

Toolbar Contains a row of icons that
provide shortcuts to the menu commands
by eliminating some keystrokes.

Split Box Splits the current window into
two panes—two smaller windows that
allow different views of the same
document.

Ruler Use the Ruler to change margins,
adjust indents, and change the width of
newspaper-style and table columns.

Text Area The text area is
where you type text and insert
tables and graphics.

Scroll Bars Use the horizontal scroll
bar to move the text from side to
side within the window. Use the
vertical scroll bar to move forward
and backward in the document.

1.2 To Choose Menus

The choice between using a mouse or a keyboard to make menu selections not only depends upon your having a mouse, but also upon which is the fastest under different circumstances. For example, this author finds that it is faster to use the keyboard for various tasks such as saving a document if making that choice while entering text. On the other hand, if the last action involved moving a block of text to a new location, then the mouse is more convenient.

If you have a mouse, you can select various menus from the menu bar by moving the mouse pointer into the menu bar and clicking the menu name. However, one advantage of learning how to use the keyboard commands to access a menu item is that you learn the letter sequences associated with menu paths.

To open a menu and choose a command by using the keyboard, follow these steps:

1. Press Alt. The Control-menu box for document button becomes darker.

2. Type the underlined letter in the name of the menu you want to open. To open the Table menu, for example, press A.

Word for Windows displays the menu. To choose a command from the menu, type the underlined letter in the command or press an arrow key to point to (highlight) the command and then press ↵Enter.

If you open a menu and then change your mind, you can do any of the following:

- Close the menu by pressing Esc two times.
- Open a different menu by pressing Esc one time and then pressing the underlined letter in the menu name.
- Open a different menu by pressing ← or → to point to (highlight) the menu name.

About Menu Sequences

In this book, instructions for giving a command or making a menu selection will take the form shown in this example: Select **File Open**. Notice that there are two highlighted letters, the **F** in File and **O** in Open, both of which correspond to underlined letters that appear in their menu names, **File** and **Open**.

It will require two steps to complete this particular command, selecting the File menu and then selecting the Open command. For convenience and clarity, we refer to these steps as a *menu sequence*.

Take the following steps to complete this menu sequence:

1. Select the File menu either by clicking on it with the mouse or by holding down the ⎡Alt⎤ key and pressing the highlighted letter **F**.

2. Select the Open command either by clicking on it with the mouse or by pressing the highlighted letter **O**.

You may use either the keyboard or the mouse to complete any menu sequence according to your own personal taste.

Learning about Menu Sequences

In this exercise, you will select various menu commands and features by entering a menu sequence. This is a sequence of letters preceded by the ⎡Alt⎤ key. Remember to use the ⎡Esc⎤ key to select another menu item.

Example:

Menu selection: **View Ruler**

Purpose: Display or hide the ruler.

Complete the exercise by using the menu sequence, **V,R**.

1. Menu selection: **Tools Thesaurus**

    Purpose: To activate thesaurus

2. Menu selection: **File New**

    Purpose: To create a new document

3. Menu selection: **Tools Options**

    Purpose: To set options

4. Menu selection: **Help Help Index**

    Purpose: To show the help index

5. Menu selection: **Help Learning Word**

    Purpose: To start the Word for Windows tutorial

1.3 To Use Dialog Boxes

When you choose the menu commands that are followed by an ellipsis (...), you will see how Word for Windows displays a *dialog box* where you supply additional information. Each dialog box is different and may contain any or all of the following types of options:

A *list box* contains a list of options and it may be open when the dialog box appears. To choose an option from either type of list box, click the option or press ← or →to point to the option and then press ↵Enter. If the list box is not long enough to display all the available options, hold down ← or →to move beyond the options that appear in the box.

The **Print** list box in the Print dialog box is an example of a *pull-down list box* and is closed when the dialog box appears. To open a pull-down list box, click the down arrow at the right end of the box or hold down Alt and type the underlined letter in the list box name.

- An *option button* is a small round button you use to choose one option from a group of related options. A black dot appears in the button of the current option. To choose an option button, click the option button or hold down Alt and type the underlined letter in the option name.

- A *check box* is a small square box you use to choose an option. It differs from an option button in that you can choose more than one check box from a group of related options. An X appears in the check boxes of the activated options. To choose a check box, click the check box or hold down Alt and type the underlined letter in the option name. To deactivate the option and remove the X from the box, choose the check box again.

- A *text box* is a rectangular box where you enter text. When a dialog box opens, the current text is usually selected. To replace the selected text, just type the new information.

- A *command button* is an oblong button that performs an action. The **OK** button accepts the settings in the dialog box. The Cancel and Close buttons cancel your changes to the settings in the dialog box. To choose a command button, click the button or highlight the button and press ↵Enter.

- A *tunnel-through command button* is a command button that opens another dialog box. To choose a tunnel-through command button, click the button, highlight the button and press ↵Enter, or hold down Alt and type the highlighted letter in the option name. In the Print dialog box, the Setup button and the Options button are tunnel-through command buttons.

Identifying Dialog Box Components

Press the menu sequence **F P** to open the File menu and choose the **Print** command. The **Print** dialog box appears. Using the dialog box on your screen and the descriptions listed in Section 1.3, fill in the blanks on the following illustration, Fig. 1.2, with the correct descriptions.

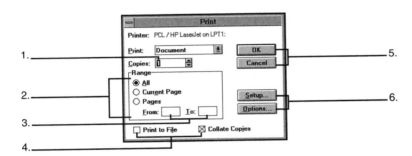

Fig. 1.2
The Print
Dialog Box.

1.4 To Get Help

To activate general **Help**, select **Help Index**.

When you activate general **Help**, Word for Windows displays the Word Help Index in the Word Help window.

From left to right at the top of the Word Help window are the Control menu buttons, the Word Help window's title bar, and the Minimize and Maximize buttons. Just below the title bar is the Help menu bar. The boxes below the Help menu bar are Help buttons. Help information appears below the Help buttons.

To print a topic you view in Help, choose the Print Topic command from the File menu. Word for Windows prints the topic that appears in the Help window. You cannot, however, print part of a topic.

When you view topics, you see topics that have solid underlines and topics that have dashed underlines. If you choose a topic that has a solid underline, Word Help jumps to the help information on that topic. If you point to a topic that has a dashed underline and hold down the left mouse button, Word Help displays a box that contains a brief definition of the word(s) you have chosen.

The Browse Forward and Browse Backward buttons are available whenever Word Help has topics before or after the current topic. The Browse Forward button displays the next screen. The Browse Backward button displays the preceding screen.

You can use the Search button to search for Word Help topics by using *keywords*.

When you choose the Search Help button, Word for Windows displays the Search dialog box in which you either type a keyword or choose one from the list box. After you type or choose a keyword, choose the Show Topics button.

You can get help about any Word for Windows command by selecting that command and pressing F1.

1. Enter the menu sequence **F,A**.

2. Press F1.

3. Read the help information.

4. Press Alt + **F,X** to close the Help window.

5. Press Esc to leave the Save As command on the File menu.

6. Enter the menu sequence **F,O**.

7. Repeat steps 1–3.

This time, help provides information on the fields within the opened dialog box. You can also get this kind of help about the Ribbon by positioning the insertion point in the Style, Font, or Point Size text boxes and pressing F1.

In addition, you can get help about using help. To get information about how Word Help works, choose the Using **Help** command from the Help window's Help menu.

Activating Help

You want to know how to underline text in a document and will use Help to locate step-by-step instructions. You can use the mouse or the keyboard with equal proficiency and will use the following steps to accomplish this task.

1. You want to activate help. You use the menu sequence __, __.

2. You are using the mouse and you want the help window to fill the entire screen. You use the mouse to click on the _____ button at the far right end of the _____ _____.

3. You are using the keyboard and you want the help window to fill the entire screen. You press the key combination <_____>+<_____> to activate the _____ _____ menu. You select the menu command, _____.

4. Since the subject you are seeking information about starts with the letter, U, from Word Help Index, you select _____ Listing Under Step-by-Step Instructions.

5. From the topic information on underlining, you learn that you can underline selected text by pressing the key combination, <_____>+<_____>.

Unit Summary

In this chapter, you learned the basics of starting Word for Windows and using the keyboard. Skill sessions also explained the parts of the Word for Windows screen, and taught how to access the menu commands, how to identify and use dialog boxes, and how to obtain on-line help.

New Terms

To review the definitions of these terms, see the glossary at the end of this book.

- Check box
- Command button
- Control-menu box for document
- Control-menu box for Word
- Dialog box
- Environment
- Insertion point
- List box

- Minimize, Restore, and Maximize buttons
- Option button
- Ribbon
- Ruler
- Scroll bars
- Split box
- Status bar
- Style area
- Title bar
- Text area
- Toolbar
- Text box
- Tunnel-through command button

Writing

2

In word processing programs such as Word for Windows, a *document* is anything that is written or printed. This means that whatever you type—from a memo or business letter to a poem or a novel—is a document. Documents can even include graphics, tables, and illustrations.

You can type a document as soon as you start Word for Windows. Although the program always gives a document a default name of Document1, you can give the new document a new name at any time.

2.1 To Start a New Document

Start Word for Windows according to the techniques you learned in Unit 1. The document which appears on-screen, Document1, is based on a document *template* called NORMAL.DOT. A template is simply a pattern that sets up the way a document will appear both on screen and when printed.

This template provides basic settings established by Word for Windows. Word for Windows provides a number of document templates that include different settings for specific tasks. The NORMAL.DOT template includes the following settings:

- A typeface with an average size (based upon typefaces available with your printer)
- Left and right margins of 1.25 inches
- Top and bottom margins of 1 inch
- Single-spaced paragraphs aligned flush with the left margin
- Tab stops set every .5 inch

Objectives

2.1 To Start a New Document

2.2 To Enter a Document

2.3 To Save the Document File

2.4 To View a Document

2.5 To Print a Document

2.2 To Enter a Document

Because of the ability to manipulate words and sentences using a word processing program, one usually speaks of entering a document as opposed to typing a document. If you change your mind about the structure of a sentence or the organization of a paragraph, you can insert words and sentences, delete phrases you don't want, and move information from one location to another.

Understanding the Insertion Point

The *insertion point* is the flashing vertical bar in the text area of the document window. In a new document, the insertion point appears in the upper left corner of the text area. Type the following line exactly as written below:

Now is the time for all good men to come to the aid of the pary

Fig. 2.1
The screen
containing text to
be corrected.

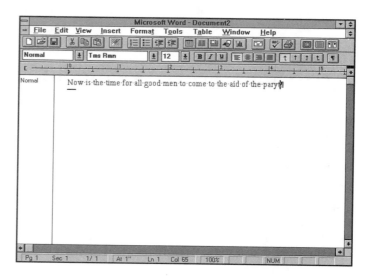

As you type, text appears to the left of the insertion point, and the insertion point moves to the right. The insertion point is the place marker for where Word for Windows inserts text into the document. You can move the insertion point by using the cursor keys on the keyboard or by pointing to a new location in the text and clicking the mouse, but you cannot move the insertion point beyond the last character in the document.

Using the Backspace Key

When you type, you may make mistakes that you notice immediately and want to correct. You can use [◆Backspace] to remove one character at a time. When you press [◆Backspace], you delete the character immediately to the left of the insertion point.

Make sure the insertion point is at the end of the line you have typed, and correct the mistake by pressing [◆Backspace] once to remove the letter, **y**. Now, type the correct letters, **t** and **y**.

Using the Delete Key

Whereas [◆Backspace] deletes the character to the left of the insertion point, the [Del] key deletes the character immediately to the right of the insertion point. Press the [←] five times and press [Del] five times to remove the word, *party*. Now, type the word, **country**, and end the sentence with a period.

Understanding Word Wrap

As you reach the end of a line, the insertion point automatically moves to the next line. This phenomenon, known as *word wrap*, occurs because Word for Windows calculates when you reach the right margin and automatically returns to the left margin. Don't press [↵Enter] until you want to start a new paragraph.

To see how word wrap works, add two spaces to the end of the sentence on your screen and add the following sentence:

> "Let our object be, our country, our whole country, and nothing but our country," as Daniel Stevens once said.

Understanding Insert and Overtype Modes

When you first open a Word for Windows document and start typing, you are in *Insert mode*. As you type, Word for Windows inserts the characters to the left of the insertion point. Any text already on-screen moves to the right. If you want to replace text that appears on-screen, you can change to *Overtype mode* by pressing [Ins].

1. Press the [Ins] key now.

2. Observe the status bar. The indicator OVR appears at the right end of the status bar.

15

3. Using your cursor keys or your mouse, move the insertion point the first **S** in the name **Stevens**.

4. Type the name **Webster**.

5. Press Ins again to return to Insert mode.

The Ins key acts as a "toggle" switch. Press Ins one time to change to Overtype mode. Press Ins again to change back to Insert mode. OVR appears on the status bar only when Word for Windows is operating in Overtype mode. This indicator disappears from the status bar when you toggle back to Insert mode.

Entering Text

With this exercise, you are beginning a continuing project that you will use throughout the text as you learn how to edit, format, and print various documents.

Use +Backspace to erase the two sentences that you have entered at this point. Now enter the following document:

Your Name
Address
City, State, ZIP

Finnegan Pin Manufacturing Company
Sales Department
123 East Michigan Avenue
East Hanover, NJ 07754

April 15, 1993

Dear Sirs:

We own a Little Jiffy Tractor and Mower, Model 107KX with an optional home garden plow attachment, Model 12PL-D. Unfortunately, we have lost the Finnegin pin that is required to assemble the plow to the tractor.

Although the Little Jiffy company is no longer in business, we found a listing of parts and manufacturers in the original instruction book that came with the tractor. According to the parts books, the Finnegin pin required is size 8R, Part No. 123-100.

If you still manufacture this part or have any in stock, we would like to order one as soon as possible. You can bill us directory or send an invoice for prepayment, whichever is most appropriate.

Thank you for your attention to this matter.

Yours truly,

Your Name

2.3 To Save the Document File

The document you create or edit in a window of a word processing program is stored in the computer's memory. When you turn off your computer or exit from Word for Windows, the portion of the computer's memory which holds the document is erased.

If you want to keep your document between word processing sessions, you must save the document to a file. It is also advisable to save your document periodically while editing since a power loss could result in your losing any changes you have made since the document was last saved.

You can save documents by choosing a command from the menu. The File menu provides three commands for saving documents:

> The Save Command
>
> The Save As Command
>
> The Save All Command

The Save As dialog box always appears when you save a new document by choosing the Save or Save As command from the File menu. The Save As dialog box also appears when you save an existing document by choosing the Save As command from the File menu.

You must provide a name (of up to eight characters) for the document In the File Name text box. You can add a three-character extension (separated from the name by a period), but if you do not type an extension, Word for Windows automatically adds the DOC extension to the file name you type.

You can change the drive and directory where Word for Windows will save the document. Because Word for Windows can convert documents to other file formats, you can also save the document in another format.

Fig. 2.2
The Save As dialog
box.

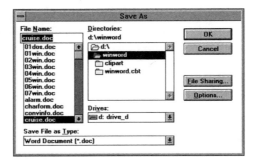

If you choose the **Options** command button, Word for Windows displays
the Save Options dialog box, which contains the default options for saving
documents.

Fig. 2.3
The Save Options
dialog box.

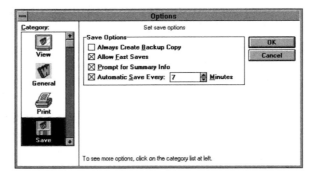

The Save Options dialog box provides the following check boxes:

Always Create **Backup** Copy saves the current version of the document
and keeps the preceding version in a file with the same name but with
the extension **BAK.**

Allow **Fast** Save saves only the changes you made since the last time you
saved.

Automatic **Save** Every check box automatically saves the document
according to the schedule you specify in the **Minutes** text box. This
option is particularly valuable to guard against data loss from power
failures—the only work you lose is the work you did since the last
automatic save.

Prompt for Summary Info prompts you for summary information each time you save a new document. If you enter summary information when you save each document, you make searching for documents easier.

Fig. 2.4
The Summary Info dialog box.

In the Summary Info dialog box, you can type up to 255 characters in the Title and Subject text boxes. Your name should already appear in the Author text box because you supplied your name when you installed Word for Windows. You can also enter key words that appear in the document (in the Keywords text box) and comments about the document (in the Comments text box). Later, you can search for documents by using the information you enter in the Title, Subject, Author, and Keywords text boxes.

If you choose the Statistics button, Word for Windows displays the Document Statistics dialog box, which contains such information as when you created and last saved the document.

Saving a New Document

To save the current document, follow these steps:

STEPS

1. Open the File menu.

2. Choose the Save As command. The Save As dialog box appears.

3. Position the cursor in the File Name text box and enter the name, LETTER. This will create the name, LETTER.DOC, for your document file.

4. Look at the box under Drives. The letter shown in this box is the drive to which your document will be saved. If the drive shown is not correct, select this box and enter the correct drive letter.

5. Look at the list under Directories. Make sure the directory that your document will be saved to is highlighted. If not, select the directory by double-clicking on your choice. If you are saving to a floppy disk, the directory will appear as a:\ or b:\.

6. Select OK or press ⏎Enter.

7. The Summary Info dialog box will appear. Enter a title: **Order Letter**; subject: **Lost Finnegan pin**; key words: **Little Jiffy tractors**; and comments: **word processing exercise**.

8. Choose OK to save the document (whether or not you typed any summary information).

Saving an Existing Document

After you save a document the first time, you can save the document again (to the same name, drive, and directory) by choosing the Save (or Save **As**) command from the File menu. If you watch the status bar, you see the percentage saved increase to 100 percent as Word for Windows saves the document.

Deciding Whether To Choose the Save or Save As Command

The Save **As** command provides choices that the Save command does not; you can specify the drive and directory where you want to store the document, the document type, and the access rights of other users. When you need to change these options, choose the Save **As** command from the File menu.

The Save All Command

The Save All command (also on the File menu) is used when you are working with more than one document at a time and you want to save all the documents.

2.4 To View a Document

Word for Windows can display several different views of the same document. You can use these views to focus on various aspects of a document and to make editing easier. You can display a document in the following four views.

Normal

In Normal View, you can see character and paragraph formatting; alignment; tab stops; and line, section, and page breaks. Normal View is the default, and generally the most useful, view. You probably will do the majority of your work in Normal View.

To change to Normal View, you open the View menu, and choose the Normal command. If a dot appears to the left of the Normal command when you open the View menu, you are already in the Normal View.

Outline

In Outline View, you can create an outline from the headings in a Word for Windows document. (Examples of headings in your text include: 2.2 To Enter a Document, Understanding the Insertion Point, Using the Backspace Key, Using the Delete Key, and Understanding Word Wrap.)

To change to Outline view, you open the View menu and choose the Outline command.

Page Layout

The Page Layout View is used to inspect and make changes to the appearance of a document. You can see all the document's formatting—including headers, footers, footnotes, columns, and frames—in their correct positions. You can edit and format text in Page Layout View.

To change to Page Layout View, you open the View menu and choose the Page Layout command. (If a dot appears to the left of the Page Layout command when you open the View menu, you are already in Page Layout View— you don't need to choose the command.)

Print Preview

When you choose the Print Preview command, you see a version of the document that appears exactly as it will print, but reduced to fit on-screen. You cannot (and are not intended to) read the text. Using Print Preview enables you to check the alignment and placement of information on the page.

To change to Print Preview, you open the File menu and choose the Print Preview command.

Enlarging or Reducing the View

You can enlarge the view of a document if you want to examine the text or graphics more closely. You can also reduce the view of the document if you want to see more text or graphics on-screen at one time. You use the Zoom feature to enlarge or reduce the view.

To enlarge or reduce a document on-screen, you open the View menu and choose the Zoom command.

The Zoom dialog box appears.

Fig. 2.5
The Zoom dialog
box.

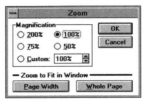

To enlarge or reduce the view by a percentage, you can choose a Magnification option button: **200%**, **100%**, **75%**, or **50%** (of Normal View size) or **Custom** (a custom size from 25 to 200 percent).

You may also change the view so that the widest line on the page fits in the window by choosing the **Page** Width button.

If you wish to see the entire page on-screen, you may reduce the text by choosing the **Whole Page** button.

Experiment with the different options to see how the current document appears in the various modes. When you finish, return your document to the normal size in the normal view.

Changing Views

In this exercise, you will view your current document, LETTER.DOC, in different views. Using the menu sequences described above, display LETTER.DOC in each of the following views:

1. Page Layout

    Try the menu selection: **View/Page** Layout

2. Outline

TIP

3. Print Preview

   Which menu would you use to print a document?

4. Zoom, 75% of Normal size

5. Normal

2.5 To Print the Document

You can print the active document by choosing the **Print** command from the File menu.

Before you print, you may want to choose the Print Preview command from the File menu to see a reduced version of the document layout. Or, you may want to change to the Normal View to see the character and formatting information.

You use the menu sequence **File/Print** to open the Print dialog box and begin the printing process.

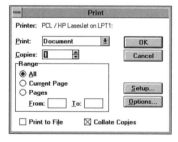

Fig. 2.6
The Print dialog box.

In the Print dialog box, you can also specify the number of copies to print, the range of pages to print, whether to collate multiple copies, and whether to print to a file (rather than on paper). The **Setup** and **Options** command buttons open dialog boxes that contain printer setup and default printing options.

The Print list box provides choices between Document, Summary Information, Annotations, Styles, Glossaries, and Key Assignment. To print the entire document, you usually use the default, Document.

Printing the Active Document

Follow these steps to print the active document, LETTER.DOC:

1. Open the **File** menu.

2. Choose the **Print** command.

3. From the Print list box, choose **Document**.

4. Choose **OK** to print the document using the default options.

Word for Windows displays messages on-screen to indicate which page is currently printing.

Unit Summary

In this chapter, you learned how to work with new documents in Word for Windows. You have learned how to start a new document, type in information, how to save your document, how to display your document in different views, and finally, how you can print out a hard copy.

New Terms

To review the definitions of these terms, see the glossary at the end of this book.

- Document
- Document template
- Word wrap
- Insert mode
- Overtype mode

Retrieving and Revising a Document

3

To make changes to an existing document, you must retrieve the document file. When you open the file, a copy of the document is loaded into a document window where you edit any portion and cut or copy selected text that can then be moved to another location. You can also delete any text you choose.

You open an existing document by choosing a command from the File menu.

1. Start Word for Windows and open the File menu.

2. Choose the Open command.

   The Open dialog box appears.

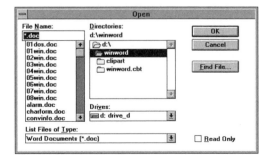

Objectives

3.1 To Move about a Document

3.2 To Select and Move Text

3.3 To Spike Text

3.4 To Copy and Paste

3.5 To Delete and Undo

Fig. 3.1
The Open dialog box.

A list of the files with the .DOC extension appears in the File Name list box.

3. You want to open the file you created in Chapter 2, LETTER.DOC. Choose this name from the File Name list and then choose OK.

   If the name of the document you want to open does not appear in the File Name list box, the file may be stored on a different drive or in a different directory. Choose the correct drive from the Drives list box and the correct directory from the Directories list box.

3.1 To Move about a Document

In order to revise a document, you must move the insertion point to the portion of the document you wish to edit.

Mouse Method: You can move the insertion point to any point on the document screen simply by clicking on that location with the mouse.

If the document is longer than the window, click the mouse on the vertical scroll bar at the right side of the window to display another part of the document. To use this bar to scroll the document,

- up or down one line, click on the up or down arrow.
- up or down one screen, click between the up or down arrow and the box.
- up or down in general, drag the box up or down.

Keyboard Method: You may also use the arrow keys on your keyboard to move the insertion point and scroll the document. To move the insertion point,

- left or right by character, press ← or →.
- left or right by word, press Ctrl+← or Ctrl+→.
- up or down by line, press ↑ or ↓.
- up or down by paragraph, press Ctrl+↑ or Ctrl+↓.
- up or down by screen, press PgUp or PgDn.
- top or bottom of current screen, press Ctrl+PgUp or Ctrl+PgDn.
- beginning or end of a line, press Home or End.
- beginning or end of the document, press Ctrl+Home or Ctrl+End.

Basic Editing

Editing involves moving the insertion point to a particular location in the text and then making your changes.

Follow these steps to locate the insertion point and conduct a simple editing step:

1. Using either the mouse or the keyboard, position the insertion point just to the left of the colon in the salutation, Dear Sirs:, in the document, LETTER.DOC.

2. Press the ⌷Del⌷ key.

3. Type a comma. The salutation should now read, Dear Sirs,.

Complete the following activities to practice moving the insertion point and Editing.

1. One of the sentences in this document has a misspelled word. The sentence begins, "You can bill us directory . . .." Change the word *directory* to directly.

2. Locate the sentence that begins, "According to the parts books, ..." The word *books* should be singular, not plural. Remove the letter *s*.

3.2 To Select and Move Text

You must identify the text you want to change *before* you can change it. To identify the text you want to change, you *select* the text by highlighting it.

Moving text involves removing, or *cutting*, the text from its current location and placing, or *pasting*, it in a new location. You move text by selecting the text you want to move and then choosing the Cu**t** and **P**aste commands from the **E**dit menu.

Mouse Method: One of the easiest ways to select text using the mouse is to click the beginning or the end of the text and then drag the mouse pointer to the other end of the text you want to select. Word for Windows highlights the text as you select it.

Using the Mouse to Select Text

Complete the following steps to practice using the mouse to highlight text.

1. Using the vertical scroll bar, position the document, LETTER.DOC, so that the paragraph beginning "If you still . . ." is fully visible in the window.

2. Move the mouse pointer to the letter *I* in the word *If*. Click and hold down the left mouse button.

3. Drag the mouse pointer to the period at the end of the sentence, highlighting the text of the sentence as you move the pointer.

4. Release the left mouse button. The text remains highlighted.

5. To unselect the selected text, click anywhere else in the document window.

Keyboard Method: The same keys that are used to move the insertion point can be combined with the ⟨⇧Shift⟩ key to highlight text. For example, the left arrow key moves the insertion point one character to the left. If you hold down the ⟨⇧Shift⟩ key at the same time, that character will be highlighted.

Use the appropriate key commands to move the insertion point to the text you want to highlight, and then use the same commands combined with the ⟨⇧Shift⟩ key to select the desired text.

Moving Text

When you move text from its current location, you use the Cut command from the Edit menu to temporarily store that text in a *Clipboard* and the Paste command from the same menu to place the text in a new location.

The Clipboard is a holding area supplied by Windows where Word for Windows temporarily places the information you cut. The Clipboard can hold only one entry at a time; each time you place information on the Clipboard, you wipe out any information previously stored there. You can place information on the Clipboard from many Windows programs and then move or copy it to other Windows programs.

STEPS The steps required to move text are:

1. Move the insertion point to the letter *M* in the phrase *Model 107KX*, in the first sentence of the document, LETTER.DOC, that begins, "We own a . . .."

2. Select the text, Model 107KX, and the space that follows it.

3. Open the Edit menu.

4. Choose the Cut command.

   Word for Windows removes the text from the document and stores it on the Clipboard.

5. Move the insertion point from its previous location to the immediate left of the letter *L*, in the word *Little*, in the same sentence.

6. Open the **Edit** menu again.

7. Choose the **Paste** command.

   The text appears in the new location. Move the insertion point to and delete the comma that follows the word *Mower*. The sentence should now begin, "We own a Model 107KX Little Jiffy Mower with an optional . . .."

Selecting and Moving Text

EXERCISE

1

Change the last three paragraphs of the document LETTER.DOC by moving the text so that the new paragraphs read as follows:

Although the Little Jiffy company is no longer in business, we found a listing of parts and manufacturers in the original instruction book that came with the tractor. According to the parts book, the Finnegin pin required is size 8R, Part No. 123-100. If you still manufacture this part or have any in stock, we would like to order one as soon as possible.

You can bill us directly or send an invoice for prepayment, whichever is most appropriate. Thank you for your attention to this matter.

Add or delete the appropriate spaces so that the moved sentences fit correctly in their new positions.

TIP

3.3 To Spike Text

While the *Spike* can be considered analogous to the Clipboard, the Spike can hold more than one entry at a time. You can repeatedly select information and place it in the Spike without losing previously selected text.

Use the Spike when you need to move information from several different locations to one new location. When you retrieve the text from the Spike, the text blocks appear in the same order that you cut them to the Spike and are separated by paragraph marks. Also, when you retrieve text from the Spike, you can leave the text in the Spike or clear the Spike.

Complete these steps to practice moving text with the Spike:

STEPS

1. Move the insertion point to the left of the space that precedes the letter *o* in the word *or* in the sentence that begins, "You can bill us directly . . .."

2. Highlight the word *or* and the space that follows it.

3. Press Ctrl + F3

   The selected text—*or*—disappears from the document, and Word for Windows adds it to the Spike.

4. You can now repeat Steps 1 and 2 for each block of text you want to move. Move the insertion point to left of the letter *b* that begins the word *bill* in the phrase, "You can bill us . . .," in the same sentence. Highlight the text *bill us directly* and include the space that follows the word *directly*.

To insert the text and empty the Spike:

1. You now position the insertion point where you want to insert the contents of the Spike. *Special Spike Rule:* The insertion point should be at the beginning of a line or preceded by a space. In this activity, move the insertion point to the immediate left of the letter *f* in the phrase *for prepayment* in the same sentence.

2. Press Ctrl + ⇧Shift + F3

   The text stored in the Spike appears in the new location, and Word for Windows deletes the text from the Spike. Delete the paragraph mark so that the sentence now reads, "You can send an invoice or bill us directly for prepayment, whichever is most appropriate."

There may be occasions when you want to repeat a word or phrase at several points in the document.

STEPS

To insert the text without emptying the Spike, you would follow these steps:

1. Place the insertion point where you want to insert the text.

2. Type **spike**.

3. Press F3.

   The text stored in the Spike appears in the document, but also remains in the Spike. If you repeat steps 1 through 3, the same text appears in the document again. If you move more text to the Spike, Word for Windows adds that text to the text already stored in the Spike.

30

Spiking Text

1. Use the document, LETTER.DOC, and restructure the sentence in the last activity to read: "You can send us an invoice for prepayment or bill directly, whichever is most appropriate."

   Remember the *Special Spike Rule*.

2. Locate the sentence that begins, "According to the parts book, the . . .." Change the end of the sentence to read, "Part No. 123-100, size 8R."

   Think about the comma first.

3.4 To Copy and Paste

Copying text involves making a duplicate of the text, *copying*, and placing the duplicate in a new location, *pasting*. Unlike moving text in which you "cut" the original text from its location, copying allows the original text to remain in its current location while you place a copy in a new location.

Copying text is similar to cutting text except that you use the Copy and **Paste** commands from the Edit menu instead of the Cut and **Paste** commands.

Using the Edit Menu To Copy Text

Locate the sentence that begins "If you still manufacture . . ." and use the Copy and **Paste** commands from the Edit menu to change it to "If you still manufacture Part No. 123-100, size 8R, or have any in stock, we . . ." Save your new version of the document LETTER.DOC when you complete this exercise.

Copying Text between Documents

In Word for Windows, you view and work on documents in windows. You can open up to nine documents at the same time, each in its own window. By default, Word for Windows maximizes the document window so that only one of the open windows is visible at a time. The *active window* is the window that contains the document on which you are currently working and, thus, the insertion point. You can type and edit text in the active document only.

To open more than one Word for Windows document, you open each document just as you open a single document. You use Ctrl + F6 to switch between active windows.

Without closing the document window that contains LETTER.DOC, you will open a second document window to enter another letter, LETTER2.DOC. The second letter contains several parts that are identical to the first. Rather than retype these common passages, copy the duplicate information from LETTER.DOC to LETTER2.DOC.

LETTER2.DOC:

Your Name
Address
City, State, ZIP

Finnegan Pin Manufacturing Company
Sales Department
123 East Michigan Avenue
East Hanover, NJ 07754

May 15, 1993

Dear Sirs:

We were delighted to receive your recent letter and to learn that you do indeed stock Finnegan pins for the Little Jiffy Tractor and Mower, Model 107KX with an optional home garden plow attachment, Model 12PL-D.

However, while we understand that you normally only sell the pins in quantities of a dozen, we really only need one, maybe two at the most. If there is any way to accommodate a single order, that is what we would prefer, but if not, then we will go ahead and take a dozen since we are that desperate.

In addition, the Finnegin pin required is size 8R, Part No. 123-100, not size 6R.

Thank you for your attention to this matter.

Yours truly,

Your Name

3.5 To Delete and Undo

In Unit 2, you learned how to delete a few characters by pressing ⎙Backspace⎙ or ⎙Del⎙. When you need to delete more than a few characters at a time, you

can select the text you want to delete and then press ⏎Enter, ⬅Backspace, or
Del. Word for Windows also provides keyboard shortcuts for deleting blocks
of text without selecting the text.

Table 3.1 lists key combinations for deleting text.

Table 3.1 Deleting Text	
Key combination	*Effect*
⬅Backspace	Deletes the selected text or deletes one character to the left of the insertion point.
Ctrl + ⬅Backspace	Deletes one word to the left of the insertion point.
Del	Deletes the selected text or deletes one character to the right of the insertion point.
Ctrl + Del	Deletes one word to the right of the insertion point.
Ctrl + X or ⇧Shift + Del	Deletes the selected text and stores the deleted text on the Clipboard.
Ctrl + Z	Reverses the last action (also known as "undo").

Using the Undo Feature

You can undo the preceding action and restore deleted text by using Word for
Windows' *Undo* feature.

To undo the preceding action by choosing a menu command, follow these
steps:

STEPS

1. Open the Edit menu.

2. Choose the Undo command.

   Because Word for Windows keeps track of your actions, the words
   next to Undo change, depending on what you are trying to undo. If
   you cut some text and then open the Edit menu, for example, the
   Undo command is Undo Cut.

33

Unit Summary

In this unit, you learned how to open an existing document, how to move around in a document, and how to use basic editing techniques to make changes to a document.

New Terms

To review the definitions of these terms, see the glossary at the end of this book.

- Select
- Clipboard
- Cut
- Copy
- Paste
- Spike
- Window
- Scroll bars

Using Editing Tools

4

When you create long documents, you often need to search a document for text, special characters, or formatting and sometimes replace the text, special characters, or formatting with other information. This allows you to make the same changes throughout a document without having to repeat the changes at each location.

The built-in editing tools, the Thesaurus, Spelling Checker, and Grammar Checker all allow you to refine and polish your document.

4.1 To Search and Replace

Often, when you review a document, you discover that you need to find—and possibly change—certain information. The Find command enables you to search for text, special characters (such as paragraph or tab marks), or formatting (such as bold or italic). The Replace command enables you not only to find this information, but also to replace it with other information. This chapter describes how to search for and replace text, commonly used special characters, and formatting.

Prepare for the exercises in this chapter by starting Word for Windows and loading the document file, LETTER3.DOC. If this document is not available on your system, you will have to enter it and then save it.

Objectives

4.1 To Search and Replace

4.2 To Find the Right Word

4.3 To Spell It Right

4.4 To Say It Right

LETTER3.DOC

Your Name
Address
City, State, ZIP

John Anderson, President
Finegan Pin Manufacturing Company
123 East Michigan Avenue
East Hanover, NJ 07754

November 12, 1993

Dear Mr. Anderson

I am taking the unusual step of writing directly to you, the president of
Finegan Pin Manufacturing Company, because we are up to our ears in
Finegan pins.

We must have lost our original Finegan pin when we moved into our
new home last spring. In any event, when we tried to attach the home
garden plow to our Little Jiffy Tractor and Mower, we discovered the
Finegan pin was missing, which, as you know, is the key to holding the
plow on the frame.

Since the Little Jiffy company has gone out of business, I wrote your
company in April and ordered a replacement Finegan pin. In early May,
we received a shipment of one case containing a dozen Finegan pins,
along with a bill.

I called your sales department and explained that we had received a
dozen Finegan pins but had actually only ordered one. I was told there
was no problem, to pay for the one Finegan pin I wanted, and that
arrangements would be made for the return of the 11 Finegan pins left
over.

In the meantime, we assembled our Little Jiffy Tractor and Mower,
attached the plow, and planted a garden. The new Finegan pin worked
just fine.

About two weeks later, a delivery truck arrived to collect the box I was returning, but it also dropped off a shipment of 12 cases of Finegan pins, along with a bill. I must admit I was awestruck, having never seen a gross of Finegan pins in one place before.

This time, I called your customer service department and spoke to a Mrs. Jones who was horrified at the mistake and averred that it must have been some sort of computer error. In any event, she said arrangements would be made for the delivery company to pick up the shipment.

It must have been about mid-June when the next delivery truck came because the California peppers were already blossoming and the tomatoe plants were about six inches high and still growing. I wasn't here at the time but my teenager signed for the shipment, which I probably would have refused. You can imagine my surprise when I came home from work to find 144 cases of Finegan pins stacked in my living room.

Well, since each case contain a dozen Finegan pins, that makes a grand total of 1,728 Finegan pins—less the one we used, of course—now stored in our guest bathroom, and to make matters worse, you have now sent us a bill for $14,532.14. Sir: We didn't order all these Finegan pins, we don't want all these Finegan pins, and we can't afford to pay the bill.

Please see what you can do about this as soon as possible as we don't want to damage our credit rating and our house guests are complaining.

Yours very truly,

Your Name

Finding Text, Special Characters, or Formatting

Follow these steps to search a Word for Windows document for text, special characters, or formatting:

STEPS

1. Open the Edit menu.

2. Choose the Find command.

   The Find dialog box appears.

Fig. 4.1
The Find dialog
box.

3. In the Find What text box, type the text or special characters for which you want to search. Type **California**.

4. Choose the Find Next button.

Word for Windows finds and displays the first occurrence (after or before the insertion point) of the information you specified.

If Word for Windows reaches the end (or beginning) of the document without searching the entire document, a dialog box asks whether you want to continue the search. To stop the search, choose the Cancel button.

Special Characters and Formatting

You can also use keyboard shortcuts to specify special character or formatting information. Table 4.1 provides a list of frequently used special characters and formats; for a complete list, see the *Word for Windows User's Guide*.

Table 4.1 Searching for Special Characters and Formatting	
Key Combination	*Searches for*
^t	A tab mark
^p	A paragraph mark
^n	A line break
^?	A question mark
Ctrl + U	Any underlined text
Ctrl + B	Any boldfaced text
Ctrl + I	Any italic text
Ctrl + D	Any double-underlined text

Replacing Text, Special Characters, or Formatting

You can find and replace text, special characters, or formatting in part or all of a Word for Windows document. To limit the area of the document in which Word for Windows finds and replaces the specified information, select the part of the document you want to search before you start the process. Otherwise, Word for Windows searches forward from the insertion point, and you can replace any or all occurrences of the information throughout the document.

To search for and replace text, special characters, or formatting, follow these steps:

1. Open the Edit menu.

2. Choose the Replace command.

   The Replace dialog box appears (see fig. 4.2).

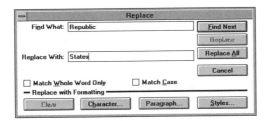

Fig. 4.2
The Replace dialog box.

3. In the Find What text box, type the text or special characters for which you want to search. Type **Finegan.**

4. In the Replace With text box, type the text or special characters you want to substitute. Type **Finnegan.**

5. Choose the Find Next button.

   Word for Windows finds and displays the first occurrence (after the insertion point) of the information you specified.

6. To replace this text, select the Replace button.

7. Word displays the next occurrence of the text you specified.

4.2 To Find the Right Word

You can use the Thesaurus to find *synonyms*, *antonyms*, and related words as you are creating or editing a Word for Windows document.

39

Using the Thesaurus

To use the Thesaurus, follow these steps:

1. Position the insertion point on or immediately before or after the word for which you want to find synonyms, antonyms, or related words. Try the word *horrified*.

2. Open the Tools menu.

3. Choose the Thesaurus command.

Word for Windows selects the word and opens the Thesaurus dialog box.

In the Thesaurus dialog box, the word for which you want to find a synonym appears in the Synonyms For box. Possible meanings of the word appear in the Meanings list box. The synonyms for the highlighted meaning appear in the Synonyms list box, and the first synonym in the list appears in the Replace With text box.

4.3 To Spell It Right

You can use the Spelling Checker to check a single word, a selected block of text, or an entire document. Word for Windows uses a standard dictionary to check spelling. When the Spelling Checker encounters a word that is not in this dictionary, you can correct the word or add it to a custom dictionary.

Follow these steps to use the Spelling Checker:

1. Position the insertion point where you want to begin checking. To check the spelling in a block of text, select the block of text.

2. Open the Tools menu and choose the Spelling command.

When Word for Windows finds a word that is not in the standard dictionary (or the available custom dictionaries), the program highlights the word and opens the Spelling dialog box.

The Not in Dictionary text box contains the highlighted word. The Change To text box contains the first word from the Suggestions list box.

You can choose any of the following in the Spelling dialog box:

The Ignore button ignores the highlighted word and continues.

The Ignore All button ignores *any other occurrence of the same word* in the document.

40

Highlight a word from the Suggestions list box and then choose the Change button to replace the highlighted word in the document with the word from the Suggestions list box.

The **Change All** button. Word for Windows replaces the highlighted word *and all other occurrences of the same word* in your document with the word from the Suggestions list box.

Choose the **Delete** button (usually the Change button) to delete one occurrence of a duplicated word (for example, "to to").

Type what you think is the correct spelling for the word in the Change To text box and choose the **Suggest** button. Word for Windows displays similar words in the Suggestions list box. If the correct spelling of a word does not display in the Suggestions list box, type the word in the Change To box and select Change.

You can choose the Cancel button or press Esc to stop checking spelling at any time.

How do you spell tomatoe?

TIP

4.4 To Say It Right

The Grammar Checker helps you to identify sentences that have questionable style or grammatical structure. For many grammatical errors, the Grammar Checker suggests corrections. By default, the Grammar Checker uses grammar and style rules for business writing, checks spelling, and provides readability statistics after checking the grammar. To change these and other options for the Grammar Checker, you can choose the **Options** button in the Grammar Checker dialog box.

Like the Spelling Checker, the Grammar Checker can check all or part of a document. To check only part of a document, select the text you want to check before you start the Grammar Checker.

To run the Grammar Checker, follow these steps:

STEPS

1. Position the insertion point where you want to begin checking. To check the grammar for a block of text, select the block of text.

2. Open the **Tools** menu.

3. Choose the **Grammar** command.

    When Word for Windows finds a sentence with questionable grammatical structure or style, the program highlights the sentence and displays the Grammar dialog box.

    The **Sentence** box contains the questionable sentence. The part of the sentence that the Grammar Checker questions appears in boldface type. The **Suggestions** list box displays information about the suspected problem.

    In the Grammar dialog box, you can do any of the following:

    Make a suggested change by choosing a suggestion from the **Suggestions** list box and then choosing the **Change** button.

    Click somewhere in the document window (or press [Ctrl]+[Tab ⁀]) and then edit the sentence in the document. Word for Windows changes the **Ignore** button to the **Start** button. When you are ready to resume checking grammar, choose the **Start** button.

    Choose the **Ignore** button to make Word for Windows skip the questionable item. If the Grammar Checker found other problems within the same sentence, Word for Windows displays the next problem in the **Sentence** box.

    Choose the **Next Sentence** button to make Word for Windows skip all problems associated with the current sentence and continue checking from the next sentence.

    Choose the Ignore **Rule** button to make Word for Windows skip the current problem and all occurrences of the same problem in this document.

    Choose the **Explain** button to display the grammar rule.

    You can stop checking grammar at any time by choosing the Cancel button or pressing [Esc].

4. When you complete your changes, save the document back to your disk. It will be used again in a future lesson.

Unit Summary

In this chapter, you learned how to use proofing tools to check a Word for Windows document. Specifically, you learned how to search for specific text and how to search for and replace specific text. You were also introduced to the thesaurus, spelling checker, and grammar checker.

New Terms

To review the definitions of these terms, see the glossary at the end of this book.

- Synonym
- Antonym

Testing Your Skills 1

Correcting a Document

Each word enclosed in brackets in the following document has been spelled incorrectly. Remove the brackets and correct the word. Save the corrected document as STAR.DOC.

The Star Spangled Banner

O say, can you see, by the dawn's early [lite],

What so proudly we hailed at the twilight's last [gleeming]—

Whose broad stripes and bright [starts], through the [parlous] fight,

O'er the ramparts we watched were so [gallently] streaming?

And the rocket's red glare, the [boms] bursting in air,

Gave proof [thru] the night that our flag was still there;

O! say, does that star-spangled banner yet wave

O'er the land of the [fee], and the home of the [braves].

Moving and Copying Text

The following lines have been numbered in the order each actually appears in a paragraph from the play *Hamlet* by Shakespeare. Arrange the sentences in the proper order in a single paragraph and then remove the numbers. Save the document as HAMLET.DOC.

8. Your gambols? Your songs?

13. Prithee, Horatio, tell me one thing.

11. Quite chop-fallen?

9. Your flashes of merriment that were wont to set the table on a roar?

7. Where be your gibes now?

12. Now get you to my lady's chamber and tell her, let her paint an inch thick, to this favor she must come—make her laugh at that.

5. My gorge rises at it.

2. Alas, poor Yorick!

6. Here hung those lips that I have kissed I know not how oft.

3. I knew him, Horatio—a fellow of infinite jest, of most excellent fancy.

1. Let me see. [Takes the skull.]

10. Not one now, to mock your own grinning?

4. He hath borne me on his back a thousand times, and now how abhorred in my imagination it is!

Creating a Business Letter

One of the most frequent uses of a word processing programming is to write business letters. Enter the following business letter, and then use the grammar and spelling checkers to correct the mistakes. Save the letter as PROPOSAL.DOC.

To:First National Intrastate Bank
133 East West Parkway
Lake Hopatcong, NJ 07444
Attention:John Handly Smirk, Vice President
Loan Department

This is a proposel for starting a new business.

While in the seafood section of a grocery store recently, I noticed a lobster tank filled with live lobsters. Tragicly, however, many lobsters were damaged—missing claws, cracked shells, dangeling antenna.

The seafood manager told me that damaged lobsters were his single biggest expense in running the seafood department, in as much as impared lobsters seldom can be sold and have to be converted to lobster salad, which is only half as profitible as an otherwise first-class lobster.

This information gave me an idea for an entirly new business—one in which there was little if any competion and tremendos opportunity. I am proposing to start a lobster repair business. To start the business, I will need to borrow $7,500. This money will be used for lobster repair materials, a lobster hospital, and a second-hand truck for transpertation.

One of the major assets of the lobster repair business is the recent developsment of a new, rust-colored, water-resistent lobster-shell glue. I have secured a protected territory from the manafacturer in order to maintain a competitive advantage.

Yours very truly,

your name

Accenting Characters

5

Changing the appearance of certain text in a document by using italics, boldface, underlining, or indenting certain words or phrases can make a document more attractive. All of these techniques fall in the general category of *Formatting*. Word for Windows divides formatting into three categories: character formatting, paragraph formatting, and page formatting. Within each category, you can format text in many ways.

5.1 To Choose Attributes

Characters are letters, numbers, punctuation marks, and symbols. When you format characters, you specify their appearance. In Word for Windows, you can change the font, point size, style, color, and placement of characters. You can also use hidden characters to insert nonprinting text into a document. In addition, Word for Windows makes it easy to insert symbols and fractions into a document.

Word for Windows enables you to apply character formatting by using the Ribbon, the keyboard, or the Character dialog box. The Character dialog box provides the most options although as you become more experienced, you may find that applying character formatting by using the Ribbon or the keyboard is often faster than using the dialog box.

Objectives

5.1 To Choose Attributes

5.2 To Size to Fit

5.3 To Go in Style

5.4 To Insert Symbols

To complete the activities and exercises in this unit, load the document WACKO.DOC. If this file is not available, then enter the document as follows and save as WACKO.DOC.

WACKO.DOC

20% Free

Wacko's Finest Nuts

Don't Surrender to Hunger Pains. Say, Nuts!

Beat the Battle of the Bulge. Say, Nuts!

Don't Go Crazy between Meals. Say, Nuts!

20% Less Fat

20% Less Cholesterol

20% More Nuts Absolutely Free

Guaranteed: Up to 80% Peanuts in Every Can

The Wacko Nut Company
Eatoour, ILL

5.2 To Size to Fit

A *font* is a complete set of type in one size and one style. Each font has a distinctive look or typeface and a family name, such as Courier or Dom Casual. Because Word for Windows supports *WYSIWYG* (What You See Is What You Get), you must consider two types of fonts: screen fonts and printer fonts. Screen fonts display text on-screen; printer fonts actually print the text. For Word for Windows to display *and* print a font correctly, both the screen font and the printer font must be available.

Most fonts are available in a range of sizes. You measure the size of a font in *points* (one point is equal to 1/72 inch); smaller point sizes produce smaller text. In Word for Windows, you can use point sizes from 4 to 127 points in .5 point increments, but Word for Windows can display *and* print a point size correctly only if that point size is available for *both* the screen and printer font.

To print Word for Windows documents, you can use the "hardware" fonts and point sizes available on your printer (the fonts supplied with your printer or the fonts you added to your printer by using font cartridges) or you can use "software" fonts (if your printer supports them).

You can choose a font and point size before you type the characters, or you can type the characters, select them, and then choose a font and point size. You can choose the font and point size by using the Ribbon or the Character dialog box.

Using the Character Dialog Box to Change the Font or Point Size

Make sure the document, WACKO.DOC is loaded. This is the text for an advertisement for a snack food product, and your task is to turn the text into an attractive advertising format. You do this by using different fonts, sizes, and character attributes, such as boldfacing and italics.

The product name probably should be in a large type and boldfaced. Special lines, such as the line that appears above the product name, might look attractive in italics. Items that are similar should be in the same font and size. The name of the company and its location can be kept small since this is not the focus of the advertisement.

TIP

The first thing you will consider in designing your ad is the font and point size of various lines.

To change the font or point size by using the Character dialog box, follow these steps:

STEPS

1. Position the insertion point where you want to change the font or point size, or select the characters for which you want to change the font or point size.

2. Open the Format menu shown in figure 5.1.

   The Format menu contains the Word for Windows formatting commands.

Fig. 5.1
The Format menu.

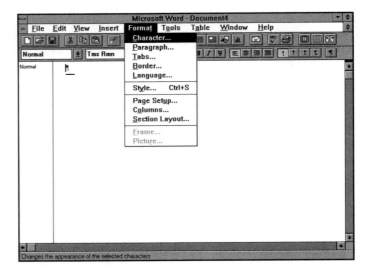

3. Choose the **Character** command.

   The Character dialog box shown in figure 5.2 appears.

4. From the **Font** list box, choose one of the available screen or printer fonts.

Fig. 5.2
The Character
dialog box.

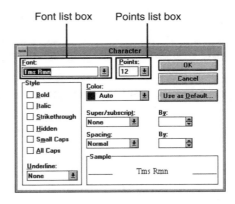

5. From the **Points** list box, choose one of the available point sizes.

   The Sample box displays the character formatting changes as you choose them. Watch the text in the Sample box to see how the text in the document will look.

6. Choose OK to accept the font or point size and return to the document.

7. Repeat until you have selected all of the fonts and point sizes for your advertisement.

5.3 To Go in Style

You can use character styles to enhance the appearance of text in many ways. In Word for Windows, you can create text in the following styles:

Table 5.1 Character Styles	
Character Style	*Effect*
bold	Characters appear in boldface type.
italic	Characters appear in italic type.
~~strikethrough~~	Characters appear as though they should be removed from the text.
Hidden	Characters do not appear on-screen unless you choose to display them or print unless you choose to print them. See Chapter 9 for information on setting the hidden text default options.
SMALL CAPS	Characters are all uppercase, but the first character of each word is the assigned point size and the rest of the characters have a slightly smaller point size.
ALL CAPS	Characters are all uppercase.
<u>single underline</u>	Both words and spaces are underlined.
<u>word</u> <u>underline</u>	Words are underlined, but spaces are not.
<u>double underline</u>	Both words and spaces have a double underline.
Character Case	The first character of each word is uppercase.

Using the Character Dialog Box to Change Character Styles

In the Character dialog box, you can specify the bold, italic, strikethrough, hidden, small caps, all caps, and underline styles. You can also apply a color to the characters.

Follow these steps to select and assign character styles.

1. Position the insertion point where you want to change the character styles or select the characters for which you want to change the character styles.

2. Open the Format menu.

3. Choose the **Character** command.

   The Character dialog box appears.

4. In the Style box, you can choose from the **Bold, Italic, Strikethrough, Hidden, Small Caps,** and **All Caps** styles. Because these styles have check boxes, you can choose more than one style at a time.

   When you choose a style, an X appears in its check box.

5. To underline the characters, choose Single, Words Only, or Double from the Underline list box.

6. To apply a color to the characters, choose a color from the **Color** list box. On-screen, you see only those colors that your monitor can display.

7. Choose OK to accept your formatting changes and return to the document. (Choose Cancel to ignore your formatting changes.)

Assigning Character Styles

Examine the advertisement WACKO.DOC, and decide how you would like it to appear. What typefaces and sizes would make it more appealing? Now that you have selected the fonts and sizes for your advertisement WACKO.DOC, you can assign various character styles to each line.

5.4 To Insert Symbols

Word for Windows also makes it easy for you to insert symbols and special characters.

Follow these steps to insert symbols and special characters.

STEPS

1. Position the insertion point where you want the symbol or special character to appear.

2. Open the **Insert** menu.

3. Choose the **Symbol** command.

   The Symbol dialog box appears.

   In the Symbol dialog box, you see characters available for the character set shown in the Symbols From list box.

   You can change the available symbols and special characters by choosing a different character set from the Symbols From list box.

4. Choose the symbol or special character you want to insert (by pressing an arrow key or by clicking) and then choose OK. You can also double-click the symbol instead of choosing the character and then choosing OK.

Creating a Bulleted list

EXERCISE

2

There are three lines in your advertisement that end in the words, "Say, Nuts!" Turn these lines into a bulleted list by placing a symbol in front of each line. Save your advertisement and print out a hard copy. Is it attractive? Appealing? Does it make you feel like a nut?

Unit Summary

In this chapter, you learned about the many ways you can format characters in Word for Windows. You learned how to apply character formatting by using the Ribbon, the keyboard, and the Character dialog box. You also learned how to insert symbols and special characters.

New Terms

To review the definitions of these terms, see the glossary at the end of this book.

- Character formatting
- Font
- Ribbon
- WYSIWYG

6

Shaping Paragraphs

Objectives

6.1 To Keep Tabs

6.2 To Indent Text

6.3 To Align Text

6.4 To Apply Spacing and Pagination

In addition to the character formatting options discussed in Unit 5, another way to improve the appearance of a document is through formatting paragraphs. You can set and align tabs, indent and align paragraphs, set line spacing, and use other options in the Paragraph dialog box.

In Word for Windows, the word *paragraph* has a special meaning: a paragraph is not necessarily a series of related sentences, but rather is any amount of text or graphics followed by a *paragraph mark*.

Fig. 6.1
The Paragraph Mark button on the Ribbon.

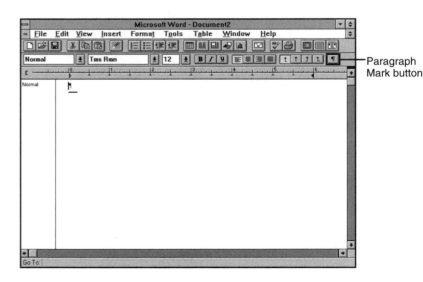

To display paragraph marks, choose the Paragraph Mark button from the Ribbon.

Word for Windows stores all *paragraph formatting* in the paragraph mark at the end of the paragraph. If you move, copy, or delete a paragraph mark, you also move, copy, or delete the paragraph formatting of that paragraph.

You can control the following attributes of paragraph formatting:

- Tab stops and tab alignment
- Indentation
- Paragraph alignment
- Line spacing

The Paragraph dialog box provides the most complete way to format paragraphs because it includes all the paragraph formatting options. Although using the Ribbon or the Ruler is faster than using the Paragraph dialog box, fewer paragraph formatting options are available on the Ribbon and the Ruler.

Paragraph Formatting

You will use the document, MEMO.DOC, to complete the steps and exercises in this unit. It consists of a sales memo that explains the shortage of Finnegan pins, production plans and schedules to meet a perceived market demand, and the introduction of a new plastic model.

Your task is to turn this sales memo into an attractive document that the sales representatives would be proud to show potential customers.

Start Word for Windows and load the document, MEMO.DOC. If it is not available on your system, then enter it exactly as it appears below:

MEMO.DOC

Finnegan Pin Manufacturing Company
123 East Michigan Avenue
East Hanover, NJ 07754

Memo: To Distribution

From: John Anderson, President

Date: December 10, 1993

Re: Shortage of Finnegan Pins

Due to a recent upsurge in orders for Finnegan pins, we regret to inform our sales staff and customers that all future orders for Finnegan pins will be delayed for approximately three months while we retool and modernize our Finnegan pin factory in East Kobunk, Alabama.

As you know, we originally closed the Finnegan pin division in the Spring of 1979 when changing economic conditions combined with the demise of both civilian and military orders substantially reduced the market for the double-flanged pins.

In recognition of our position as the market leader in this product and conscious of our responsibility to our customers, however, we did stockpile several thousands of these pins in our South Billings, NH, warehouse. Frankly, we anticipated that the quantity stored would last well into the next century.

However, in recent months, the demand for Finnegan pins has completely emptied our warehouse, and while we have not yet determined exactly how these pins are being used, we are certain that the high quality we have always maintained in our product has resulted in customers finding new uses for these versatile and sturdy pins.

Accordingly, and in keeping with our commitment to meeting market demands in a timely and efficient manner, we are installing a new, computerized production line at the East Kobunk facility that will manufacture more than 100 Finnegan pins a minute. In addition, we will soon have the capacity to produce ten different sizes of the Finnegan pin, from 2R to 20R, which, of course, includes the popular size, 8R.

Finally, we are adding a new, plastic Finnegan pin that will be manufactured to the same high quality of our aluminum and steel Finnegan pins. The new plastic pin also will be available in a single flange model as well as the standard double flange.

Finnegan Pin Features:

Split shank for maximum flexibility allows insertion in odd-shaped or off-sized latching couplers.

Easy-grip grasp ring designed for both manual and automatic tool insertion.

Self-regulating tension loops eliminate the requirement for separate compression rings.

Impact-resistant holdbacks that hold tight for centuries.

Color-coded for quick identification in strategic couplings.

Seal-coated for long life; a pin for the generations.

Finnegan Pin Production Schedule:

Date; Size Availability

Plastic; Aluminum; Steel

3/12/94; 2R, 4R; 2R; 2R

3/27/94; 6R, 8R; 4R, 6R; 4R

4/2/94; 10R; 8R; 6R, 8R

4/9/94; 12-20R; 10R, 12R; 10R

4/16/94; -; 14-20R; 12R

4/23/94; -; -; 14-20R

We trust that these release dates will meet our customers' needs and reestablish FPMCo as the premier manufacturer of Finnegan pins. Orders will be accepted beginning Jan. 5, 1994.

6.1 To Keep Tabs

Often, you don't want all the text in a document to begin at the left margin— for example, you may want to indent the first line of each paragraph. In Word for Windows, you use tab stops to position text at locations other than the left margin. When you press Tab⁵, the insertion point moves to the next tab stop, and a tab character →⌋ appears in the space (if you are displaying tabs).

Word for Windows provides default tab stops at half-inch intervals from the left margin. You can delete a default tab stop or change the distance between default tabs, but to make other changes, you must create a *custom* tab stop. (To delete a default tab stop, set a custom tab to its right. When you set a custom tab, Word for Windows deletes all default tabs to the left of the custom tab.)

Default tabs are left-aligned, which means that when you press Tab⁵ and then type, the text you type flows toward the right margin. For custom tabs, you can specify the alignment of text (left, center, right, or decimal) relative to the tab stop. Text you type from a center tab is centered around that tab. Text you type from a right tab flows back toward the left margin. A decimal tab, which you use to align columns of numbers, combines a right tab and a left tab. Text flows toward the left margin until you type a period (.), which represents the decimal point in a number. Then, text flows toward the right margin.

Fig. 6.2
Tab alignment
in Word for
Windows.

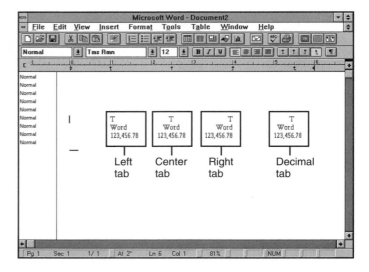

Here, you can see the effect on text and numbers of choosing left, center, right, or decimal tab alignment. Each T indicates the position of a custom tab stop.

You can also fill the space before a custom tab stop with dots, dashes, or underscore characters (known as *leader characters*).

STEPS

To set custom tab stops and alignment by using the Tabs dialog box, follow these steps:

1. Position the insertion point where you want to begin using the tab stops, or select the paragraphs to which you want to add the tab stops.

2. Open the Format menu.

3. Choose the **Tabs** command.

    The Tabs dialog box appears.

4. In the Default Tab Stops list box, you can change the interval between default tabs. Normally, the default tab stops are set at half-inch intervals.

5. To set a custom tab, type its position relative to the left margin (in inches, by default) in the **Tab** Stop Position text box.

Figure 6.3
The Tabs dialog box.

6. To align text or numbers at the custom tab stop, choose **Left**, **Center**, **Right**, or **Decimal** from the Alignment box. The default option button is **Left**.

7. To fill the space preceding the custom tab with dots, dashes, or a line, choose an option from the Leader box.

    When you press Tab ⇥, Word for Windows will fill the space before the leader tab stop with the leader character.

8. After you set the position, alignment, and leader (if any) for the custom tab, choose the **Set** button to store the custom tab setting.

    When you set a custom tab, Word for Windows deletes all default tabs to the left of the custom tab.

9. Repeat steps 5 through 7 to set additional custom tabs.

10. Choose OK to accept the tab stop settings or Cancel to ignore them.

To clear a custom tab, choose it from the **Tab Stop Position** list box and then choose the **Clear** command button. To clear all custom tabs, choose the **Clear All** command button. (The **Set** and **Clear** command buttons are available only when a custom tab position appears in the **Tab Stop Position** text box.)

Using the Tabs Dialog Box To Set Tab Stops and Tab Alignment

There is a production schedule in your document, MEMO.DOC, that should be customized using tab stops. You can also add character formatting to further enhance the schedule. Here is one suggested design:

Finnegan Pin Production Schedule

Date		Size Availability	
	Plastic	Aluminum	Steel
xxxxx	xxxxx	xxxxxx	xxxx

Use the Tabs Dialog box to format the production schedule in MEMO.DOC. Save your work, and print out a hard copy when done.

6.2 To Indent Text

Rather than indenting just the current line of text, you can position an entire paragraph at a particular tab stop. Word for Windows enables you to create a variety of indents, including hanging indents. (You often use hanging indents, which align the first line of the paragraph at the left margin and indent subsequent lines of the paragraph to the next tab stop, in bibliographies.)

Using the Keyboard To Set Indentation

One section of MEMO.DOC contains a list of Finnegan pin features. One way to feature this list is to apply the techniques you learned in Unit 5 to underline the heading and place bullets in front of each item on the list. In addition, you can use a *hanging indent* to further define the items in the list.

A hanging indent is one in which the first line of the paragraph is the normal width of the paragraph (including any paragraph tabs and adjusted for margins), but all subsequent lines of the same paragraph are indented.

To create a hanging indent for each of the items in the features list, use the following shortcut:

1. Position the insertion point where you want to begin indenting, or select the paragraphs you want to indent.

2. Press Ctrl + T. Word for Windows indents all lines except the first line to the first tab stop.

   If you want to align the body of the paragraph at the next tab stop, press Ctrl + T again. Word for Windows leaves the first line at the left margin and indents the rest of the paragraph to the next tab stop.

To move the body of the text to the preceding tab stop, press Ctrl + G.

Using the Paragraph Dialog Box To Set Indentation

You can also use the Indentation box on the Paragraph dialog box shown in Fig. 6.3 to indent from the left or right margin or indent the first line.

You can choose indentation measurements from the From **Left**, From **Right**,

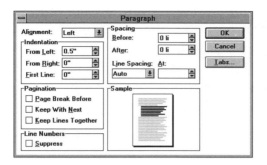

Fig. 6.4
The Paragraph
dialog box.

or **First** Line list boxes, or you can type measurements in the boxes. Word for Windows sets the indentations relative to the left margin. If you choose indentation measurements from the list boxes, watch the Sample box as you scroll through the list. The picture in the Sample box changes to simulate the current choice. If you type measurements in the boxes, click one of the other boxes in the Paragraph dialog box to change the Sample box picture.

Use the From **Left** list box to specify the distance you want to move *all* text from the left margin. Use the From **Right** list box to specify the distance you want to move text from the right margin. You can also indent a paragraph's first line differently from its other lines. Use the **First** Line list box to specify the distance you want to move the first line of a paragraph from the *left indent setting* (not the left margin). You can create hanging indents by changing the First Line setting to the negative equivalent of the From **Left** setting.

If you change the From **Left** list box to .5 inch and leave the From **Right** and First Line settings at 0, all lines in the paragraph will be indented .5 inch from the left margin.

You can create a hanging indent by setting the From **Left** list box to .5 inch and the **First** Line list box to -.5 inch.

Indenting MEMO.DOC

Use the Paragraph dialog box to set indentation for the rest of MEMO.DOC. Open the Format menu and choose the **Paragraph** command.

EXERCISE
2

61

6.3 To Align Text

In Word for Windows, you can align text to the left margin, center text, align text to the right margin, or justify text.

Aligning text to the left margin produces a ragged right margin.

Centering text between the margins makes both margins ragged.

Aligning text to the right margin produces a ragged left margin.

Justifying text aligns the text to both margins by expanding the spaces between words.

Using the Keyboard To Set Paragraph Alignment

While you can use the Alignment box in the Paragraph dialog box, you also can control paragraph alignment by using just the keyboard. Using MEMO.DOC, try each of the following to see the effect.

To align text to the left, press Ctrl+L.

To center text, press Ctrl+E.

To align text to the right, press Ctrl+R.

To justify text, press Ctrl+J.

6.4 To Apply Spacing and Pagination

You can control line spacing through paragraph formatting, both within and between paragraphs. You can, for example, single space lines within a paragraph, but double space between paragraphs. You can control line spacing only by using the Paragraph dialog box.

To set line spacing, position the insertion point where you want to change the line spacing and open the Paragraph dialog box. In the Spacing box, you can control the amount of space before a paragraph, after a paragraph, and within a paragraph.

From the Before and After list boxes, you can choose (or type) the number of lines you want before or after a paragraph. From the Line Spacing list box, you can choose the amount of vertical space Word for Windows uses for each line. If you choose Auto, each line is as tall as the tallest character in the line. The Single, 1.5 Lines, and Double options set line spacing at one line, one and one-half lines, and two lines, respectively. The At Least option enables you to set a minimum spacing between lines. The Exactly option enables you to set a specific line spacing in the **At** list box (such as 1.25 lines or .75 line—you can choose a number from the list or type a number).

Pagination

Because Word for Windows includes page sizes, font sizes, line spacing, and top and bottom margin settings, the program calculates when you fill a page with text. Whenever you fill a page, Word for Windows inserts a "soft" page break. Sometimes these soft page breaks occur in places where you don't want them (for example, in the middle of a list). You use the options in the Pagination box to prevent unwanted soft page breaks within paragraphs. You can move the page break before a selected paragraph (**P**age Break Before), or you can force two paragraphs to appear on the same page by preventing a page break between them (Keep With Next). You can also prevent a page break within a paragraph (**K**eep Lines Together).

Printing MEMO.DOC

Examine the alignment and appearance of each of the paragraphs you are using for MEMO.DOC, and adjust them so that each is clean and striking in appearance.

The final step in producing an attractive sales memo is to adjust your line spacing to accommodate your character size and to insert your page breaks so that reading the document is both easy and pleasing. Use the techniques described in this section to complete your layout and print out a hard copy.

Don't forget to save your document back to disk in order to preserve your changes.

In Unit 3, you learned about Page Layout View and Print Preview.

Unit Summary

In this chapter you learned about the many ways you can format paragraphs in Word for Windows. You learned about the paragraph attributes available for formatting and how to apply paragraph formatting by using the dialog boxes, the keyboard, the Ribbon, the Ruler, and the Toolbar. You learned how to remove, repeat, and copy formatting.

New Terms

To review the definitions of these terms, see the glossary at the end of this book.

- Paragraph
- Paragraph mark
- Paragraph formatting
- Ribbon
- Ruler

Designing Pages

7

In the previous two units, you discovered that documents convey much more than simple information. Documents convey impressions. You can enhance any document by accenting certain information—formatting characters and paragraphs to make details easy to read or understand.

You have seen reports and long documents that have been divided into sections for clarity and ease of reading. This book is an example of such a document. It is divided into sections that include the title pages, table of contents, individual units, and the index. In this unit, you will learn how to format pages and sections. Specifically, you will learn how to set margins, paper size, and orientation; use page numbering; and insert section breaks.

When you first open a document, Word for Windows provides basic default settings. These default settings include the following:

- Left and right margins of 1.25 inches
- Top and bottom margins of 1 inch
- A typeface of average size
- Single-spaced paragraphs aligned to the left margin
- Tab stops set every half-inch.

In Unit 5 you learned how to change the font (typeface) and point size; in Unit 6 you learned how to change the paragraph alignment and spacing and the tab stops. Now, you will learn how to change the page formatting.

Objectives

7.1 To Set Margins

7.2 To Control Pagination

7.3 To Insert Page Numbers

7.4 To Create Sections

7.1 To Set Margins

By changing margin settings, you can affect the document's length, improve the clarity of the document, or leave room for binding the document. As you will learn later in this chapter, you can also divide a document into different sections, and each section can have its own set of margins.

To complete the exercises in this chapter, load the document file, MEMO.DOC, and make sure your insertion point is in the upper left corner of the typing area of your screen.

Setting Margins by Using the Page Setup Command

You have the most flexibility when you change margins by using the Page Setup command. You can choose the portions of the document you want to affect: selected text, the current section, all text from the insertion point forward, or the entire document.

If you choose to affect the selected text or the text from the insertion point forward, Word for Windows inserts section breaks. New sections always begin on a new page. You can also set up a "gutter" margin to provide extra space for binding the document or set up margins for "facing pages" so that you can assemble the document as a book.

1. Select the Page Setup command from the Format menu. The Page Setup dialog box shown in figure 7.1 appears. Margins is the default page attribute option.

Fig. 7.1
The Page Setup
dialog box.

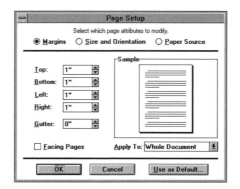

2. Set the margins, including any gutter margin, by typing margin measurements in the **Top**, **Bottom**, **Left**, **Right**, or **Gutter** text boxes or by clicking the arrows at the end of the text boxes to increase or decrease the current measurement. Watch the picture in the Sample box to see the effect of your choices. If you plan to assemble the document as a book, choose the **Facing** Pages check box.

The choices in the **Apply To** list box vary depending on whether you created sections in the document and whether you selected text before opening the Page Setup dialog box.

3. Save the new margin settings in the current document template by choosing the Use as Default button. If you choose this option, all future documents based on the current template use the margins you establish here.

4. When you finish setting the margins, choose OK to accept your choices or Cancel to ignore them.

Setting Margins for MEMO.DOC

One way to make the document, MEMO.DOC, more attractive is to provide enough "white" space (areas of the document that contain no printing) to eliminate any aspect of clutter. Large blocks of printed type tend to appear gray and adding white space in strategic areas breaks up the gray.

At the same time, however, you do not want too much white space. Extremely wide left and right margins can detract from the importance of the document itself or, at the very least, make it appear to be spaced out. Using the steps described above, set the margins for MEMO.DOC according to your personal judgement of what is both attractive and substansive.

When you are done, save your file and print out a hard copy.

To see the overall effect of your changes, choose the Print Preview command from the File menu.

7.2 To Control Pagination

When formatting documents, you often need to control pagination. In this section you will learn about page breaks, repagination, and page numbering.The first step in setting pagination is to determine your paper size and its orientation. You also use the Page Setup dialog box to change the paper size and orientation and to set the paper size or orientation.

Setting Paper Size and Orientation

In many networking situations, you often have various printers to choose from depending upon the nature of the printout desired. If you are using a computer and printers on a network, you should check with your system administrator to find out what paper sizes and orientations are available.

To set paper size and orientation, follow these steps:

1. Open the Format menu.

2. Choose the Page Setup command.

    The Page Setup dialog box appears.

3. Choose the Size and Orientation option button at the top of the Page Setup dialog box.

    The dialog box changes to display size and orientation options. In the Paper Size list box, you can see the paper sizes that your printer supports.

4. Choose a paper size from the Paper Size list box or enter a custom paper size in the Width and Height text boxes (by typing the paper measurements or by clicking the arrows to increase or decrease the current measurements). Watch the picture in the Sample box to see the effects of your changes.

5. In the Orientation box, choose Portrait (normal, top to bottom) or Landscape (sideways).

6. From the Apply To list box, choose the portions of the document you want to affect. The options in this list box vary depending on whether you selected text before you opened the Page Setup dialog box. If you selected text, Word for Windows inserts section breaks before and after the selected text.

7. To save these size and orientation settings in the current document template, choose the Use as Default button. If you choose this option, all future documents based on the current template have the size and orientation you establish here.

8. Choose OK to accept your choices or Cancel to ignore them.

To see the overall effect of your changes, choose the Print Preview command from the File menu.

Setting Page Breaks

Because Word for Windows calculates page sizes, font sizes, line spacing, and margins, the program can determine when you have filled a page with text. Whenever this occurs, Word for Windows inserts a "soft" page break in the document. As you edit or move text, Word for Windows continually recalculates the amount of text on each page and moves the soft page breaks accordingly.

Occasionally, you may want to begin a new page in a specific location. To do this, you insert a "hard" page break. Hard and soft page breaks differ in two ways:

- Word for Windows inserts soft page breaks automatically, but you insert hard page breaks manually.
- You cannot delete a soft page break, but you can delete a hard page break.

You can insert and delete hard page breaks by using menu commands or by using the keyboard.

In this exercise, you will insert a hard page break so that the section containing the Production Schedule will appear on a separate page.

Use the menu and follow these steps to create a page break:

1. Position the insertion point just before the text you want to begin the new page.

   It would seem appropriate to include the heading: Finnegan Pin Production Schedule.

2. Open the **Insert** menu.

3. Choose the **Break** command.

4. Choose the **Page** Break option button (the default).

5. Choose OK.

Use the keyboard and follow these steps to create a page break:

1. Position the insertion point just before the text you want to begin the new page.

2. Press (Ctrl)+(↵Enter).

3. Repeat step 2 to put in another page break.

EXERCISE
2

Eliminating Extraneous Hard Page Breaks

Delete one of the hard page breaks you have just created by following these steps:

1. Select the hard page break you want to delete.

2. Open the Edit menu.

3. Choose the Cut command.

Delete the second hard page break by following these steps:

1. Select the hard page break you want to delete or position the insertion point on or immediately after the hard page break.

2. If you selected the page break or positioned the insertion point on the page break, press (Del). If you positioned the insertion point immediately after the page break, press (◆Backspace).

Repaginating

By default, Word for Windows calculates pagination in *background mode*—that is, whenever you pause while typing or editing. Background repagination uses some memory, so if you experience memory problems, you may want to turn off this option. To turn off background repagination, follow these steps:

1. Open the Tools menu.

2. Choose the Options command.

3. From the Category options, choose General.

4. Choose the Background Repagination check box to turn off this option.

   Word for Windows removes the X from the check box.

5. Choose OK.

If background repagination is off, Word for Windows stills repaginates the document whenever you do any of the following:

■ Print the document.

■ Choose the Repaginate Now command from the Tools menu.

■ Choose the Page Layout command from the View menu.

■ Choose the Print Preview command from the File menu.

■ Compile a table of contents or an index.

7.3 To Insert Page Numbers

You can put page numbers in a document by choosing the Page Numbers command from the Insert menu.

When you use the Page Numbers command, you insert a page number on all pages except *the first page*. You can choose where the page numbers appear when printed, their alignment, their format, and the starting page number. By default, Word for Windows places an Arabic number (1, 2, 3, and so on) in a footer on the right side of the page. Word for Windows begins page numbering with page 1 and numbers the pages continuously.

1. Position the insertion point where you want page numbering to begin.

2. Open the Insert menu.

3. Choose the Page Numbers command.

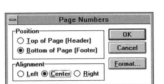

Fig. 7.2
The Page Numbers
Dialog Box.

The Page Numbers dialog box enables you to choose the position, alignment, and format of page numbers.

4. Choose the Top of Page (Header) or Bottom of Page (Footer) option button to specify the position of the page numbers.

5. Choose Left, Center, or Right alignment for the page numbers.

6. To change any default options, choose the Format button.

   The Page Number Format dialog box appears. After you make the changes, choose OK to return to the Page Numbers dialog box.

7. Choose OK in the Page Numbers dialog box to apply the page numbers to the document.

Inserting Page Numbers

Your task is to insert page numbers in the document MEMO.DOC by using the Page Numbers command and the steps shown above.

EXERCISE
3

7.4 To Create Sections

Word for Windows enables you to divide a document into sections so that you can format different portions of the document in different ways. If you want the formatting for a document to be consistent throughout the document, you do not need to create any sections—the entire document is one large section. You must create a new section, however, if you want to change any of the following formatting for just part of a document:

- The margins, paper size, or page orientation
- The format, position, or sequence of page numbers
- The contents or position of headers and footers
- The location of footnotes
- The number of newspaper columns
- The line numbering

To insert a section break, follow these steps:

1. Make sure that you are in Normal View.

2. Position the insertion point where you want to start the new section. *Hint:* The new section contains the production schedule table.

3. Open the Insert menu.

4. Choose the **Break** command.

   The Break dialog box appears.

   The default option is **Page Break.**

5. In the Section Break box, choose the page where you want the new section to begin and then choose the OK button.

Section breaks appear in the document as double dotted lines. These section marks do not print.

Word for Windows stores all section formatting in the section mark. If you delete a section mark, you delete all section formatting for the preceding section. The text then assumes the formatting of the next section.

To remove a section break, position the insertion point immediately before the section mark and press Del or immediately after the section mark and press ◆Backspace.

You can format a section by positioning the insertion point anywhere in the section and then choosing any of the following commands:

- The Page Setup command (from the Format menu)
- The Columns command (from the Format menu)
- The Section Layout command (from the Format menu)
- The Page Numbers command (from the Insert menu)
- The Header/Footer command (from the View menu)

Inserting Section Breaks

The document MEMO.DOC could be made more attractive by using different margin settings for the body of the memo than for the production schedule table.

Vertical Alignment

Changing the vertical alignment adjusts the spacing between paragraphs in a section. Word for Windows aligns the text in a section with the top margin, centers it between the top and bottom margins, or justifies by aligning the top line with the top margin and the bottom line with the bottom margin. You can create a title page, for example, by centering the text vertically on the page. Although you cannot see the effect of your choice in Normal View, you can choose the Print Preview command from the File menu to see the alignment.

To set the vertical alignment of a section, open the Format menu and choose the Section Layout command. When the Section Layout dialog box appears, select the Top, Center, or Justified option button, then OK.

Unit Summary

In this chapter, you learned how to set up documents by using page and section formatting. When formatting pages, you set margins, paper size and orientation, paper source, and pagination. You can also create bulleted or numbered lists. When formatting sections, you can insert section breaks, set vertical alignment, and turn on line numbering.

New Terms

To review the definitions of these terms, see the glossary at the end of this book.

- Portrait
- Landscape
- Soft page break
- Hard page break
- Pagination

Testing Your Skills 2

Part I Formatting a Letter

Load the document, PROPOSAL.DOC, that you created as part of Testing Your Skills 1. Edit the document and format as follows:

To: First National Intrastate Bank
133 East West Parkway
Lake Hopatcong, NJ 07444

Attention: John Handly Smirk, Vice President
Loan Department

Subject: This is a proposal for starting a new business.

The Need

While in the seafood section of a grocery store recently, I noticed a lobster tank filled with live lobsters. Tragically, however, many lobsters were damaged—missing claws, cracked shells, dangling antennae.

The seafood manager told me that damaged lobsters were his single biggest expense in running the seafood department, inasmuch as impaired lobsters seldom can be sold and have to be converted to lobster salad, which is only half as profitable as an otherwise first-class lobster.

The Concept

This information gave me an idea for an entirely new business—one in which there was little if any competition and tremendous opportunity. I am proposing to start a lobster repair business.

Funding

To start the business, I will need to borrow $7,500. This money will be used for lobster repair materials, a lobster hospital, and a secondhand truck for transportation.

Competitive Advantage

One of the major assets of the lobster repair business is the recent development of a new, rust-colored, water-resistant lobster-shell glue. I have secured a protected territory from the manufacturer in order to maintain a competitive advantage.

Marketing Objectives

- Contact area lobster dealers
- Offer an introductory trial period
- Create newspaper advertising
- Create a sales brochure
- Build reputation by quick, reliable service
- Produce quality results
- Build business base by gradually expanding into new areas

Yours very truly,

your name

Formatting and Printing

Enter and format the following memo using character, paragraph, and page formatting to highlight the significant details and create an attractive document. Save the file as MEMO2.DOC. Print a copy of your memo when done.

To: Senior Staff

Date: [Current Date]

From: [Your Name]

Re: Eliminating redundancy in general business sales

Currently, our sales force consists of three separate units: general business, corporate sales, and independent channels.

With the recent consolidation of our communications product line and the subsequent downsizing of production units, I feel that we could achieve even greater savings in our sunk costs by eliminating overlapping operations in our separate sales units.

Specifically, I am proposing that we close a number of branch offices that are producing marginal sales, consolidate separate branch units into single offices, and reduce the number of regional offices that service the branch offices.

Closings

The following general branch offices will be closed:

- Bangor, Maine
- Portland, Oregon
- Alcoa, Tennessee
- Willow Twig, Virginia

Consolidations

The following general branch offices will be consolidated with the corporate sales offices:

- Seattle, Washington
- Dallas, Texas
- Pitchman, New Jersey

Restructured

The following regional office assignments will be restructured:

From . . .   *To . . .*

1. Walla Walla, Washington   Seattle

2. Houston, Texas   Dallas

3. Elizabeth, New Jersey   Pitchman

Budget Lines and Savings

Budget lines affected and schedules savings are projected as follows:

Org. Code	1st Qtr	2nd Qtr	3rd Qtr	4th Qtr
GBS12-345	3,234.69	45,544.14	47,899.33	55,234.45
GBS14-221	105,223.45	107,336.11	112,346.44	123,377.81
COR02-101	112,333.77	114,445.34	117,678.32	121,765.09
CIR11-291	123,445.45	125,345.44	127,234.22	133,234.33
Totals	374,237.36	392,671.03	405,158.31	433,611.68

8

Working with Files

As you work in Word for Windows, you will want to use many of its facilities that will help make your work easier and more efficient. For example, there are features specifically designed to help you manage documents.

If you create many documents, some with information you want to reuse, you may find it more difficult to identify specific documents or even to remember the contents of a particular document. You will find it harder to find the one document that contains the information you need for the current report.

In this unit, you will learn how to use these features to open, delete, copy, and print one or more documents. You also will learn how to specify print options so that you can print one page or several pages of a document.

8.1 To Use Summary Information

In the Summary Info dialog box, you can store information about a document that will help you to identify the document and to find that document later. You can

- Save a title that is longer than the document name as well as subject information and keywords
- Record the author of the document and any comments about the document

Objectives

8.1 To Use Summary Information

8.2 To Find Files, Sort and Search

8.3 To Delete and Copy

8.4 To Print Files

In addition to the information you supply about a document, Word for Windows maintains certain statistics about each document: the date the document was created, the date it was last saved, the date it was last printed, and so on.

By default, Word for Windows displays the Summary Info dialog box the first time you save a document. Although entering the summary information takes a few extra moments initially, having this information can save you a great deal of time later (when you are trying to find a particular file).

Later, you may want to add to or change the summary information you supplied when you first saved the document. To edit the summary information or update the document statistics, you can open the Summary Info dialog box directly by choosing the Summary Info command from the File menu.

Updating Summary Information

Start Word for Windows and load the file, LETTER3.DOC.

To open the Summary Info dialog box, follow these steps:

1. Open the File menu.

2. Choose the Summary Info command.

   The Summary Info dialog box shown in figure 8.1 appears.

Fig. 8.1
The Summary Info
dialog box.

Summary Info		
File Name: Document1		OK
Directory:		Cancel
Title:		
Subject:		Statistics...
Author: Elaine J. Marmel		
Keywords:		
Comments:		

At the top of the dialog box, you see the DOS file name and directory for the document. You cannot change this information in the Summary Info dialog box.

You don't have to complete *every* text box in the Summary Info dialog box. The more information you include, however, the easier it will be to find the file later. In each text box, you can enter up to 255 characters of descriptive information.

3. Use the **Title** text box to enter a document name that is longer than the DOS file name. Enter **Overloaded on Finnegan Pins**.

4. In the **Subject** text box, enter a description of the document: **letter of complaint on receiving too many Finnegan pins**.

5. In the **Author** text box, enter your name.

6. In the **Keywords** text box, enter any words that represent important information or general topics in the document. You can, but don't have to, separate the words with commas; character case is not important. Enter **Finnegan, pins, gross, California, Anderson**.

7. In the **Comments** text box, fill in any other information that might help you to locate this document later. Use your imagination and enter your own comments.

8. Select OK.

Creating Summary Information

Load the document file MEMO.DOC and complete the Summary Information as if you were an employee of the Finnegan Pin Manufacturing Company.

In a large company, hundreds of memos will be written and stored in files. Eventually, document names such as MEMO001.DOC, PIN05.DOC, and PLANS.DOC, will become meaningless. Create meaningful entries for both the **Subject** and **Keywords** text boxes that will allow someone not familiar with this memo to locate it at some future date.

8.2 To Find Files, Sort and Search

By using the **Find File** command, you can view information about Word for Windows documents without opening them. You can search for documents and view and edit summary information. You can also open, print, delete, copy, and preview documents.

To open the Find File dialog box, follow these steps:

1. Open the **File** menu.

2. Choose the **Find File** command.

The Find File dialog box appears.

The first time you open the Find File dialog box, Word for Windows lists all documents stored in Word for Windows format on the current path. You can see the paths Word for Windows searched and the sort criteria at the top of the dialog box. In the File Name list box, Word for Windows lists the complete DOS path name, including any directories, for each document (so that you can see the location of the documents). By default, Word for Windows highlights the first document in the File Name list box and displays the highlighted document's contents in the Content box.

At the bottom of the dialog box are the **Open**, **Print**, **Delete**, and **Copy** command buttons you can use to manage documents and the Su**mm**ary command button you can use to open the Summary Info dialog box.

The **Open** command button performs the same function as the **Open** command on the **File** menu. The **Print** command button enables you to print one or more files. Printing is covered in detail later in this unit.

Sorting Files

The Options command button in the Find File dialog box enables you to change the way Word for Windows sorts the File Name list and what information the program displays in the Content box.

When you choose the Options command button, the Options dialog box shown in figure 8.2 appears.

Fig. 8.2
The Options dialog box that is accessed from the Find File dialog box.

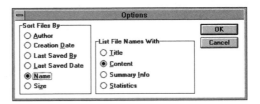

The Options dialog box is divided into two parts.

In the Sort Files By box on the left, you can choose the method Word for Windows uses to order the files in the File Name list.

In the List File Names With box on the right, you can choose what information Word for Windows displays in the Content box. If you choose Title, for example, the Content box displays *just the title of the highlighted file*. Word for Windows uses the summary information you enter to display any of the options in the List File Names With box.

Changing the Search Criteria

You can change the search criteria Word for Windows uses by choosing the Search command button.

If you choose the Search command button, the Search dialog box shown in figure 8.3 appears.

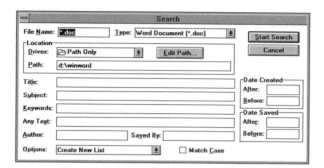

Fig. 8.3
The Search dialog box.

Most of the options in the Search dialog box are text boxes in which you can type search information.

In the File **Name** text box, you can specify the characters Word for Windows uses to search for file names. (You can use the DOS wild card characters * and ? to specify the file names.)

In the **Type** list box, you can choose a specific type of document for which you want Word for Windows to search. If you choose to search for document templates, for example, Word for Windows automatically changes the information in the File **Name** text box to *.DOT.

You also can change the location for the search by choosing a different drive from the **Drives** list box, by choosing the **Edit Path** command button, or by typing a DOS path name in the **Path** text box.

If you choose the **Edit Path** command button, the Edit Path dialog box appears.

Word for Windows can search more than one path for your criteria. To add or delete drives or directories you want Word for Windows to search, you use the Edit Path dialog box. After you choose the search paths, choose the Close button to return to the Search dialog box.

Word for Windows uses document summary information to search for any information you type in the Title, Subject, Keywords, Author, or Saved By text boxes or the Date Created or Date Saved boxes in the lower portion of the Search dialog box. Word for Windows searches the documents themselves for any text you type in the Any Text text box.

8.3 To Delete and Copy

To avoid building a clutter of old files on your disk, you should periodically delete files which you probably will not use again in the future. If you absolutely must save everything, then copy the files to a floppy disk and store in a cool, dry, dark place where they can age like vintage port.

Word for Windows also creates a back-up copy of a file each time you edit and save a document. If you do a lot of word processing, particularly creating memos and letters, the *.BAK files can accumulate like coat hangers. Efficient computing means cleaning out the *.BAK closet from time to time.

Deleting a File

The **Delete** command button enables you to delete one or more files. When you choose a file and then choose the **Delete** button, Word for Windows opens a dialog box that displays that file's complete path and file name and asks you to confirm that you want to delete the file. To delete the file, choose the **Yes** button. If you don't want to delete the file, choose the **No** button or press (Esc).

Copying a File

The **Copy** command button enables you to copy one or more files to a different directory or drive. You can use this command button, for example, if you want to copy a document to a floppy disk in drive A.

When you use the **Copy** command button, you cannot enter a new name for a file. If you want to change the name of a file, open the file and then choose the Save **As** command from the File menu. Provide a new name for the file in the Save As dialog box and save the file. Then close the original file (the one with the old name), and delete it by opening the Find File dialog box and following the directions for deleting a file.

8.4 To Print Files

You can print Word for Windows documents in many ways. You can print all of a document or part of a document. You can print more than one copy of a document. You can print more than one document at a time. You can print the summary information and statistics with the document or separately. In addition, you can print envelopes. The printing method you choose depends on what you want to print.

You can print part of the active document (or print more than one copy of all or part of the active document) by choosing options in the Print dialog box.

Confirm that the document, MEMO.DOC, is loaded in your active window. Open the Print dialog box by following these steps:

1. Open the **File** menu.

2. Choose the **Print** command.

   The Print dialog box shown figure 8.4 appears.

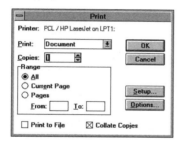

Fig. 8.4
The Print dialog box.

In the Range box, you can specify the part of the document you want to print: **All**, **Current Page**, or **From** and **To**. In the Copies box, you can type the number of copies you want to print or click the arrows to increase or decrease the current number.

By default, Word for Windows collates copies so that pages print in the correct order.

3. Choose the **Options** command button, Word for Windows displays the Print Options dialog box shown in figure 8.5.

   This dialog box displays the default print options set by using the **Options** command on the **Tools** menu.

Fig. 8.5
The Print Options
dialog box.

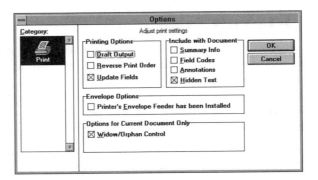

The options in this dialog box are in effect every time you print a Word
for Windows document. If you change these options, the new options
remain in effect until you change them again. Because all the options
are check boxes, you can choose more than one option at a time.

In the Printing Options box, you can choose **Draft Output**, which
prints using the printer's draft mode. The **Reverse Print Order** option
prints the pages from the last page to the first page. The Update Fields
option updates any fields in your document (such as a date field)
before printing.

In the Include with Document box, you can choose **Summary Info** to
print the summary information whenever you print a document.

In the Envelope Options box, choose the Printer's Envelope Feeder
has been installed check box only if the printer has an envelope
feeder.

In the Options for Current Document Only box, choose the **Widow/
Orphan Control** check box to prevent widows and orphans. In Word
for Windows, widows occur when the last line of a paragraph appears
alone at the top of a page, and orphans occur when the first line of a
paragraph appears alone at the bottom of a page.

4. When you finish choosing options, choose OK to return to the Print
   dialog box.

5. Select OK to print the document.

EXERCISE
2

Using the Print Dialog Box

Make the document LETTER3.DOC your active document, and use the steps
you learned above to print out a copy of the document.

Printing by Using the Find File Command

You can print documents that are not open by using the Find File command on the File menu. You also can print more than one document at a time or print the summary information for one or more documents that are not open.

To print a document that is not open, follow these steps:

1. Open the File menu.

2. Choose the Find File command.

3. Choose the document you want to print: LETTER3.DOC.

4. Choose the Print button.

Unit Summary

In this unit, you learned how to use the Summary Info command, the Find File command, and the Print command to manage and print your documents.

New Terms

To review the definitions of these terms, see the glossary at the end of this book.

- Summary information
- Keywords
- Path
- Active document
- Printer graphics resolution

9

Working in Styles

Objectives

9.1 To View and Apply Styles

9.2 To Define Styles

9.3 To Delete and Rename Styles

9.4 To Print and Save Styles

An efficient method for working with files is only one aspect of making your work environment easier. Another is eliminating many of the repetitive tasks associated with the content of the files.

Perhaps you have created a standard document such as a memo with specific character and paragraph formatting. Rather than go through the steps of applying that formatting to every memo, you can define the formatting as a style and then attach that style to every memo you write.

9.1 To View and Apply Styles

Word for Windows provides several standard styles that are available in every document, ready for you to use.

You can see the standard styles when you open the Style dialog box. To open the Style dialog box, follow these steps:

1. Open the Format menu.

2. Choose the Style command.

The Style dialog box shown in figure 9.1 appears.

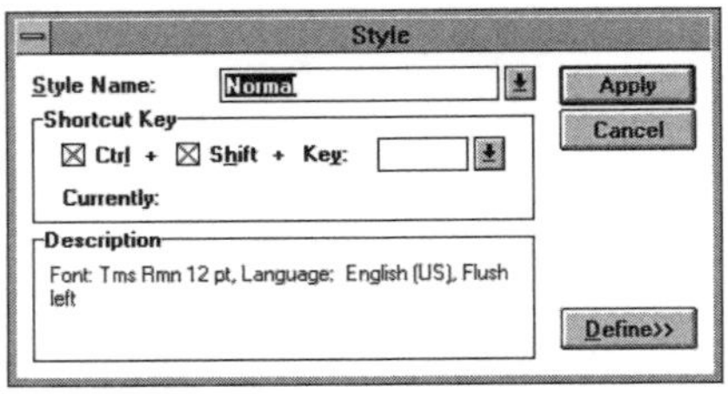

Fig. 9.1
The Style
dialog box.

The collection of styles that appear in the **Style Name** list box are the document's style sheet. If you define additional styles for the document, those styles become part of the document's style sheet. (Different documents can have different style sheets.)

To see additional standard styles in the Style dialog box, follow these steps:

1. Open the **Style Name** list box.

2. Press ⌈Ctrl⌋+⌈Y⌋.

All the standard styles appear in the **Style Name** list box.

If you highlight different styles, you can see information about the styles in the Description box. As you become familiar with the standard styles, you may not need to define styles of your own.

Applying a Style

You can apply styles by using the Ribbon or the Style dialog box. You can type the text, select it, and then choose the style, or you can choose the style and then type the text.

To apply a style by using the Ribbon, open the Style list box and choose a style.

To apply a style by using the Style dialog box, follow these steps:

1. Open the **Format** menu.

2. Choose the **Style** command.

   The Style dialog box appears.

3. Open the **Style Name** list box.

4. Choose a style.

5. Choose the **Apply** button.

Seeing the Effects of Styles

Load the document LETTER3.DOC, and follow the steps listed previously to apply various styles. As you will see, the different styles result in immediate changes to your document—some of which are appropriate while others inhibit either your message or the appearance of your document.

9.2 To Define Styles

The easiest way to define a style is to base the new style on text that has the formatting you want to save as a style. Word for Windows uses the formatted text as a "model" for the style.

To define a style based on formatted text, follow these steps:

1. Load MEMO.DOC as your current document.

2. Apply all the character and paragraph formatting you want to define as the style.

3. Select the formatted text.

4. Position the insertion point in the Style list box on the Ruler (use the mouse or press Ctrl + S).

5. Type a name for the new style. The style name can have up to 24 characters, including spaces, but cannot include the backslash (\) character. Do not use a name that already exists in the Style list. Use the name, FINN, for the style that will apply to MEMO.DOC.

6. Press Enter.

Creating a Style First

You also can use the Style dialog box to create a new style before you type the text.

Complete the steps in this activity using the name MYSTYLE so that you can practice using the delete feature next. Load the document LETTER3.DOC, and insert a new paragraph by moving the insertion point to the end of the last paragraph and pressing Enter.

To create a new style before you type the text, follow these steps:

1. Open the Format menu.

2. Choose the Style command.

   The Style dialog box appears.

3. Type a name for the new style in the Style Name text box. The style name can have up to 24 characters, including spaces, but cannot include the backslash (\) character. Do not use a name that already exists in the Style Name list. In this case, use the name MYSTYLE.

4. Choose the **Define** button.

The second Style dialog box shown in figure 9.2 appears.

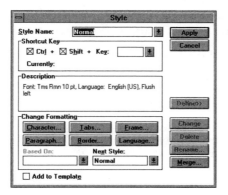

Fig. 9.2
The second Style dialog box is used for defining new styles.

5. Use the buttons in the Change Formatting box to define the formatting for the new style:

You want the style to include character formatting so choose the **Character** button to open the Character dialog box (see Unit 5 for more information on character formatting). Select a character formatting style of your choice.

You want the style to include paragraph formatting, so choose the **Paragraph** button to open the Paragraph dialog box (see Unit 6 for more information on paragraph formatting). Select a paragraph formatting style of your choice.

If you want the style to include tabs, choose the **Tabs** button to open the Tabs dialog box (see Unit 6 for more information on tabs). If you have previously applied a tab format to the paragraphs in LETTER3.DOC, then apply a similar format using this option.

6. When you finish defining the formatting for the new style, choose one of the following buttons:

   ■ The Add button adds the new style to the list without applying its formatting to the paragraph containing the insertion point. Then choose the Close button to close the Style dialog box.

   ■ The Apply button adds the new style to the list and applies its formatting to the paragraph containing the insertion point.

   ■ The Cancel button ignores the formatting choices.

Verifying A New Style

With LETTER3.DOC as your current document and by choosing the Apply button from the steps above, the paragraph marked by the insertion point now contains your newly created style. Add the following paragraph to your letter to verify that the style you created is attached to the paragraph:

> Also, as I was completing this letter, I received a telephone call from Wabash-Kennecut Railroad freight dispatcher informing me that my boxcar had arrived and was currently on a siding at the Little River Train Depot. My boxcar? Sirs, enough is enough. There simply is no room in my yard for a boxcar.

Print out a copy of your new letter showing the applied style in the new paragraph, but do not save LETTER3.DOC back to disk.

If you are using the autosave feature of Word for Windows, your document LETTER3.DOC may have been saved while you were working on it. In this case, delete the entire paragraph, including the paragraph mark at the end of the paragraph, and then save the file back to disk.

9.3 To Delete and Rename Styles

You can delete a style from the style sheet list by using the Style dialog box.

To delete the stylesheet, MYSTYLE, follow these steps:

1. Open the Format menu.

2. Choose the Style command.

   The Style dialog box appears.

3. From the Style Name list box, choose the style you want to delete, MYSTYLE, that you created earlier.

4. Choose the Define button.

   The second Style dialog box appears.

5. Choose the Delete button.

   A dialog box asks you to confirm the deletion.

6. Choose Yes.

7. Choose the Close button.

   Any text formatted with the style you deleted reverts to Normal style.

Renaming Styles

If you don't want to change the formatting of a style, you can change the name of the style instead of deleting it.

To change the style name, follow these steps:

1. Open the Format menu.

2. Choose the Style command.

   The Style dialog box appears.

3. From the Style Name list box, choose the style you want to rename.

4. Choose the **Define** button.

   The second Style dialog box appears.

5. Choose the **Rename** button.

   The Rename Style dialog box appears.

6. Type the new name in the New Style **Name** text box.

7. Choose OK.

8. Choose the Close button.

9.4 To Print and Save Styles

You may wish to print a style sheet (the style names and the descriptions that appear in the Description box of the Style dialog box).

To print a style sheet, follow these steps:

1. Open the **File** menu.

2. Choose the **Print** command.

3. From the **Print** list box, choose Styles.

4. Choose OK.

Word for Windows prints the style names and descriptions for the active document only.

Adding Styles to a Template

When you create a new style, you are creating that style for the active document. When you save the active document, you save the style *for that document only*. You may find that you want some styles you create to be available whenever you use the current template.

To accomplish this, you can add your styles to the template's style sheet.

To add a style to the current template, make sure that the document MEMO.DOC is loaded into your active window and follow these steps:

1. Open the Format menu.

2. Choose the Style command.

   The Style dialog box appears.

3. From the Style Name list, choose the style you want to add to the template's style sheet. Select FINN.

4. Choose the Define button.

   The second Style dialog box appears.

5. Choose the Add to Template check box.

Fig. 9.3
The Add to
Template check
box in the Style
dialog box.

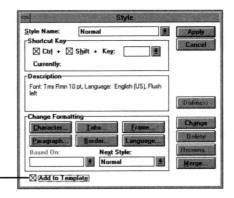

Add to Template check box ⎯⎯⎯

The Add to Template check box is at the bottom of the second Style dialog box as shown in figure 9.3.

6. Choose the Change button.

7. Choose the Close button.

Unit Summary

In this unit, you learned how to view and apply styles; how to define, delete, and rename styles; and how to save a style by attaching it to the current template.

New Terms

To review the definitions of these terms, see the glossary at the end of this book.

- Style
- Style sheet
- Standard styles
- Template
- Options

10

Featuring Templates

Objectives

10.1 To Relate
Documents
to Templates

10.2 To Choose and
Attach Templates

10.3 To Modify
Templates

10.4 To Create
Templates

When Word for Windows was installed on your computer system, the option of installing the templates was provided by Microsoft. If these templates were installed, you have available more than a dozen templates that can provide the basis for many different kinds of documents, including reports, letters, and memos.

If the templates supplied by Microsoft are not installed, you still have a template called NORMAL.DOT. As you learned in Unit 2, Word for Windows bases all new documents on the NORMAL.DOT template unless you choose a different template.

NORMAL.DOT is a special template in which Word for Windows stores items that are *globally* available—that is, items that are available for all documents, regardless of the template on which a document is based.

10.1 To Relate Documents to Templates

These templates can save you time when you format documents. Table 10.1 provides a list of the templates and the description Microsoft supplied for each template in its summary information.

Table 10.1 Document Templates	
Name	*Description*
ARTICLE2	Create an article manuscript for publication
DATAFILE	Print Merge Data/Header File Template
DISSERT2	Create an academic dissertation
FAX	Create a cover sheet for a fax
LETBLOCK	Create a block letter
LETMDSEM	Create a modified semi-block letter
LETMODBK	Create a modified block letter
LETPERSN	Create a personal letter
MAILLABL	(No description supplied-creates mailing labels)
MEMO2	Create a business memo
MSWORD	Word for DOS key mappings
NORMAL	Default template for new documents
OVERHEAD	Create a set of slides for an overhead projector presentation
PRESS	Create a press release
PROPOSAL	Create a business proposal
REPLAND	Create a business report with the pages in landscape orientation (wider than they are tall)
REPSIDE	Create a business report with sideheads (headings which are printed to the left of the text)
REPSTAND	Create a business report with the pages in standard portrait orientation (taller than they are wide)
TERM2	Create an academic term paper

Just as Word for Windows documents have the default extension DOC, Word for Windows templates have the default extension DOT.

Copying a Template

Using the techniques for copying a file that you learned in Unit 8, copy the template, FAX.DOT to MYFAX.DOT.

10.2 To Choose and Attach Templates

Whenever you create a document, you base it on a template. If you don't choose a template, Word for Windows chooses NORMAL.DOT for you. You can choose a template other than NORMAL.DOT by using the **New** command on the **File** menu.

In the New dialog box, the available templates appear in the Use Template list box.

Choose the template you want to use from the Use Template list box. If you highlight a template before you choose it, a brief description of that template appears in the Description box.

To change a template, follow these steps:

1. Open the File menu.
2. Choose the Template command.

   The Template dialog box appears.
3. Open the Attach Document To list box.
4. Choose a different template for the document.
5. Select OK.

Attaching a Document to a Different Template

Sometimes, you may start a document based on one template (such as NORMAL.DOT), then later decide that you want to use a different template.

1. Load the document LETTER3.DOC and change the template by following the steps listed above. Print out a copy of the memo to demonstrate how the document was changed.

2. Because of the urgency of your situation, you have decided it will be faster to send your letter to the Finnegan Pin Manufacturing Company by fax instead of mailing it. Attach the template MYFAX.DOT to LETTER3.DOC.

10.3 To Modify Templates

You can modify a template just as you can modify a document. You open the template, make changes to it, and then save it. Just be aware that if you type text while working in a template, you are adding that text to the template. In other words, that text becomes *boilerplate text*, which appears whenever you use the template to create a new document.

To modify a template, follow these steps:

1. Open the **File** menu.

2. Choose the **Open** command.

   The Open dialog box appears.

3. From the List Files of **Type** list box, choose Document Templates.

   In the File **Names** list box, Word for Windows displays only those files that have the extension DOT.

4. Choose the template you want to modify.

5. Choose OK.

6. Make changes to the template as you would change any document.

7. Save the template by using the **File** menu.

You can also change the character, page setup, or language formatting in a template by modifying a document based on the template.

The Character, Page Setup, and Language dialog boxes each include a Use as **Default** command button. To modify the character, page setup, or language formatting of a template, open a document on which that template is based. Then, open the appropriate dialog box, make the changes, and choose the Use as Default button.

When you choose this button, Word for Windows displays a dialog box asking you to confirm that you want to change the document template. Choose **Yes**.

Modifying MYFAX.DOT

The template MYFAX.DOT was created for a business. Since you are an individual, you will need to change the template so that it is appropriate for your letter. Following the steps listed above, load MYFAX.DOT, make the appropriate changes, and print out a faxable copy of your letter.

10.4 To Create Templates

You can create a new template in two ways:

- You can modify an existing template and then save the modified template under a new name.
- You can convert a document to a template and then save the template.

To create a new template by modifying an existing template, follow the steps for modifying a template (in the preceding section), but choose the Save **As** command from the File menu the first time you save the new template. Type a name for the new template and choose OK. Word for Windows displays the Summary Info dialog box. You can use summary information for templates just as you use summary information for documents, so take a few minutes to complete the information.

You can also choose to create a new template based on an existing template. This process is very similar to modifying an existing template. Follow these steps:

1. Open the File menu.

2. Choose the New command.

   The New dialog box appears.

3. From the Use Template list box, choose the existing template on which you want to base the new template.

4. In the New box, choose Template.

5. Choose **OK**.

6. Make any changes to the existing template.

7. Open the File menu again.

8. Choose the Save or Save **As** command.

   Word for Windows displays the Save As dialog box.

9. Type a name for the new template.

10. Choose OK.

To convert an existing document to a template, follow these steps:

1. Open the document on which you want to base the new template.

2. Make any changes, including deleting any text you don't want to include in every new document based on the template.

3. Open the File menu.

4. Choose the Save As command.

5. Type a name for the new template.

6. From the Save File as Type list box, choose Document Template (*.dot).

7. Choose OK.

Creating a Personal Template

There are many documents that are based upon standardized formats. The author frequently sends bills to his publisher and has found it useful to create a basic invoice that requires only the addition of the current date and the amount billed.

A psychology student might find a standard survey form useful. Anyone writing a thesis might find a standard bibliography form helpful for organizing information found in the library. Select one of the following ideas and create your own template. Next, create several documents using the new template to demonstrate its effectiveness.

Template ideas:

Homework assignments

Monthly letter to parents (standard request for money?)

Personal resume

Weekly shopping list

Standard bibliography for research thesis.

Book, movie, or music reviews (include ratings)

Recipes (cooking or chemical)

Sports playbook (football plays, basketball plays, etc.)

Weekly/monthly budget

Unit Summary

In this unit, you learned that Microsoft supplies various standard templates that can be related to certain types of documents; how to choose and attach templates; how to modify templates; and how to create a template.

New Terms

To review the definitions of these terms, see the glossary at the end of this book.

- Template
- Document template
- Boilerplate text

Testing Your Skills 3

Making Your Work Easier

Summary information can be critical in a working environment where many different types of documents are processed daily. Various scenarios can be developed for a wide variety of businesses, each requiring a different set of titles, categories, and keywords to identify types of documents.

For example, a real estate investment firm might have internal memos, standard sales letters to prospective clients, position letters to current clients, property lists, stockholder or limited partner lists, legal papers, purchase authorizations, sell orders, and the like. A manufacturing company would have some documents in common with the real estate investment firm—internal memos, stockholder lists, legal letters—but the manufacturing company would also have documents peculiar to its own business: cost analyses, letters to suppliers, manufacturing procedures, union procedures, purchase orders, shipping standards, and the like.

An efficient office manager will design a tracking system with file names, titles, descriptions, categories, and keywords that make locating document files easy.

Your task is to design such a system for various businesses, and create for the business a standard operating procedure document that details and describes the system. This activity requires both knowledge of the Summary Info feature and the ability to think creatively.

Example (or create your own):

Business	Type of documents used by business
Real Estate Investment	Internal memos
	Meetings and schedules
	Property lists
	Sales letters
	Client letters
	Owner (stockholders, partners) letters
	Employee procedures, rules, regulations
	Holiday, vacation
	Schedules, requests
	Purchase authorizations
	Sell orders
	Letters to attorneys
	Marketing strategies, brochures
	Letter to government regulatory agencies

Modifying Templates

The following documents should be available on your system. Modify the default templates provided by Microsoft that were used when the following documents were created, saving the templates under the suggested names. Add whatever changes you think are appropriate.

Document	Original Template	New Template
MYFAX.DOC	FAX	MYFAX.DOT
MYLET.DOC	LETPERSN	MYLET.DOT
MYMEMO2.DOC	MEMO2	MYMEMO2.DOT
MYSLIDES.DOC	OVERHEAD	MYSLIDES.DOT
MYNEWS.DOC	PRESS	MYNEWS.DOT
MYPROPO.DOC	PROPOSAL	MYPROPO.DOT

After creating the new templates, attach each new template to its corresponding document file. Next, modify the original documents according to the new templates.

Glossary

Active document. The document that contains the insertion point. Unless you have divided the screen into multiple windows, the active document is the document you are currently viewing on-screen.

Antonym. A word that means the opposite (or nearly opposite) of the original word. In some cases, the Thesaurus also finds antonyms.

Boilerplate text. Text which appears whenever you use the template to create a new document.

Character formatting. The process of specifying the appearance of letters, numbers, punctuation, and symbols. You can specify the font, point size, style, color, and placement of characters.

Check box. A small square box in a dialog box that you use to choose an option. It differs from an option button in that you can choose more than one check box from a group of related options. An X appears in the check boxes of the activated options.

Clipboard. A *holding area* provided by Windows and used by all Windows applications to store information temporarily. The Clipboard holds only one entry at a time; whenever you cut or copy information to the Clipboard, Windows replaces the preceding entry.

Command button. An oblong button in a dialog box that performs an action.

Control-menu Box for Document. A button that opens the *Control-menu Box for Document*, which allows you to switch to the next open document, to split the screen, or to change the size of the document window.

Control-menu Box for Word. A button that opens the *Control-menu Box for Word*, which controls the size of the Word for Windows application screen and includes commands for closing the current session, switching to other programs, and running other commands.

Copy. Making a duplicate of selected text. When you choose the Copy command from the Edit menu, Word for Windows places a copy of the selected text on the Clipboard. When you combine copying with pasting, you can copy text from one location to another.

Cut. Eliminating selected text. When you choose the Cut command from the Edit menu, Word for Windows removes the selected text, but stores it on the Clipboard. When you combine cutting with pasting, you can move text from one location to another.

Dialog box. A box that appears on the screen whenever Word for Windows needs additional information to complete an action.

Document. Anything written or printed.

Document template. An empty document in which Word for Windows stores standard settings such as margins, typeface and type size, tab stops, and line spacing.

Environment. The various screens, menus, icons, and commands that make up the Windows operating system or a Windows program.

Font. A complete set of type in one size and style, usually comprising alphanumeric characters and various symbols associated with a particular language.

Hard page break. A page break that you insert to force Word for Windows to begin a new page.

Insert mode. The opposite of Overtype mode. In Insert mode, existing text moves to the right as you type new text. Insert mode is the default mode for Word for Windows.

Insertion point. A flashing vertical bar that indicates where text will appear when you begin to type.

Keywords. One kind of summary information you can supply about a document. Word for Windows can search for all documents that have the keywords you specify.

Landscape. A paper orientation for which text flows across the 11-inch side of the paper from the left margin to the right margin.

List box. A box that presents a list of options within a dialog box.

Minimize, Restore, and Maximize buttons. These buttons provide a quick way to change the size of Word for Windows or the document.

Option button. A small round button in a dialog box that you use to choose one option from a group of related options. A black dot appears in the button of the current option.

Options. Default settings used by Word for Windows. The settings in the Options dialog box determine the way Word for Windows functions.

Overtype mode. The opposite of Insert mode. In Overtype mode, new text replaces existing text as you type.

Pane. A portion of a window. When you divide a window into more than one part, each part is called a pane.

Paragraph. Any amount of text ending in a paragraph mark.

Paragraph formatting. The process of specifying the appearance of paragraphs. You can specify the position and alignment of tabs, the indentation and alignment of paragraphs, and line spacing.

Paragraph mark. Shown as a symbol resembling a backwards P with a double-line backbone when visible on screen. The paragraph mark stores instructions for the formatting of that particular paragraph.

Paste. Placing the contents of the Clipboard into a document. When you combine pasting with cutting or copying, you can move or copy text from one location to another.

Path. The DOS term that represents the location of a file. The path generally consists of a drive name (such as a:, b:, or c:) and directory name(s) separated by the backslash (\) character.

Portrait. A paper orientation for which text flows across the 8 1/2-inch side of the paper from the left margin to the right margin.

Printer graphics resolution. A term that describes how clearly a document will print. Because resolution is based on the number of dots per inch (dpi), higher resolution numbers indicate better clarity.

Ribbon. The Ribbon is used to make selected text boldface, underlined, or italic; to control paragraph alignment; and to customize tab settings.

Ruler. You use the Ruler to change margins, adjust indents, and change the width of newspaper-style and table columns.

Scroll bars. You use the horizontal scroll bar to move the text from side to side within the window. You use the vertical scroll bar to move forward and backward in the document.

Select. The action you take to identify the text with which you want to work. When you select text, Word for Windows highlights it.

Soft page break. A page break that Word for Windows inserts after calculating that the text has filled the page from the top margin to the bottom margin.

Spike. Word for Windows' specialized version of the Clipboard. You can store multiple entries in the Spike.

Split box. Splits the current window into two panes—actually two smaller windows that allow different views of the same document.

Standard styles. The styles provided by Microsoft in the template NORMAL.DOT.

Status bar. Displays pertinent information about the page that contains the insertion point or about the highlighted command.

Style. A combination of character and paragraph formatting that you save in a style sheet. You can use a style, also called a *paragraph style*, to apply frequently used formatting more efficiently.

Style area. An optional feature, the *Style Area* at the left of the screen displays the name of the style for each paragraph.

Style sheet. A collection of the different styles available in a document. You can create different style sheets for different documents.

Summary information. Information you supply to Word for Windows about a document. Word for Windows can use this information when searching for documents.

Synonym. A word that means the same (or nearly the same) as the original word. The Thesaurus finds synonyms.

Text area. The text area is where you type text and insert tables and graphics.

Title bar. Displays the program name and the name of the document in which you are working.

Toolbar. The Toolbar contains a row of icons that provide shortcuts to Word for Windows menu commands by eliminating some keystrokes.

Template. An empty document in which Word for Windows stores a particular style sheet and particular character, paragraph, and page settings. You can use a template, also called a *document template*, as a pattern to create similar documents.

Text box. A rectangular box where you enter text in a dialog box.

Tunnel-through command button. A command button that opens another dialog box.

Window. A rectangular area on-screen in which you work when using a Windows program. You can open up to nine documents at one time; Word for Windows places each document in its own window. When you *maximize* a window, that window fills the screen, blocking other windows from view.

Word wrap. A concept that describes how Word for Windows automatically moves the insertion point to the beginning of a new line when you fill the current line with text.

WYSIWYG. Pronounced "Whiz-ee-wig," the acronym is taken from the first letters of the phrase "What You See Is What You Get," meaning that the image on screen is what is printed on paper providing both the screen and the printer share the same fonts.

Index

A

active document, 85
active windows, 31
aligning
    paragraphs, 62
    text, 61-62
All Caps style, 51
antonyms, 39-40
applying document styles, 89

B

background mode, 70
Backspace key, 15
boilerplate text, 99
boldface style, 51
boldfaced text, 38
Browse Backward button, 10
Browse Forward button, 10
bullets, 53

C

Cancel button, 8
capitalization, 51
centering text, 62
character styles, 51-52
characters
    attributes, 47-48
    special, finding/replacing, 35-39
check boxes, 8
Clipboard, 28
Close button, 8

colors (text), 47
command buttons, 8
Control menu box, 6, 9
controlling pagination, 67
copying
    files, 84
    templates, 98
    text, 31-32
custom tabs, 57-60
customizing templates, 101
Cut command (Edit menu), 27-29, 70

D

default settings
    documents, 65
    tabs, 57
defining document styles, 90
Delete key, 15
deleted text, restoring, 33
deleting
    files, 84
    hard page breaks, 70
    page breaks, 69
    styles, 92
    text, 33
dialog boxes, 8-9
DOC extension, 17
documents, 13
    boilerplate text, 99
    converting to templates, 101
    default settings, 65
    editing, 26-27

files
    finding, 81-82
    searching, 83-84
    sorting, 82
finding/replacing text, 35-39
hanging indents, 60
inserting characters/symbols,
  52-53
line spacing, 62
margins, 66-67
navigating, 26
page breaks, 69
pagination, 63
    controlling, 67
    hard page breaks, 69
    page numbers, 71
    repaginating, 70
    soft page breaks, 63
paper, 68
paragraphs, 54
    aligning, 62
    formatting, 55-60
    indenting, 60-61
previewing, 67
printing, 23-24, 85-86
relating to templates, 96-98
repaginating, 70
retrieving, 25-26
saving, 17-20
section breaks, 72-73
styles
    applying, 89
    defining, 90
    deleting, 92
    printing, 93
    renaming, 93
    standard styles, 88-89
    templates, 94
    verifying, 92
    viewing, 89
summary information, 79-81
tabs, 57-58

templates, 13
    converting, 100-101
    copying, 98
    customizing, 101
    modifying, 99
    selecting, 98
    switching, 98
text
    aligning, 61-62
    character styles, 51-52
    copying, 31-32
    deleting, 33
    entering, 14-17
    fonts/point sizes, 48-51
    formatting, 47-48
    indenting, 60-61
    moving, 28-29
    pasting, 31-32
    restoring deleted, 33
    selecting, 27-28
    spiking, 29-31
    vertical alignment, 73-74
    viewing, 20-23
dot leaders, *see* leaders (tabs)
double underlined text, 38, 51

E–F

editing documents, 26-27
enlarging views, 22

FAX template, 97
files
    copying, 84
    deleting, 84
    finding, 81-82
    searching, 83-84
    sorting, 82
Find command (Edit menu), 35-39
Find dialog box, 37
finding
    files, 81-82
    special characters, 35-39
    text, 35-39

fonts, 47
formatting
    characters, 47
    paragraphs, 55-57
    section breaks, 73
    style, 51
    tabs, 57-60
    text, 47-48

G–H–I

Grammar Checker, 41-42
gutter margins, 66

hanging indents, 60
hard page breaks, 69-70
Help, 9-10
hidden text default options, 51

indenting text, 60-61
Insert mode, 15-16
inserting
    hard page breaks, 69
    section breaks, 72-73
insertion point, 14
italic text, 38, 51

J-K

justifying text, 62

keyboard shortcuts, 33
keyboards
    formatting characters, 47
    navigating documents, 26-27
    selecting
        menus, 6-7
        text, 28
keywords, 10

L

landscape orientation (paper), 68
leaders (tabs), 58
left indent setting, 61
left-aligning text, 62

lines
    finding breaks, 38
    spacing, 62
list boxes, 8

M

margins
    default settings, 65
    gutter margins, 66
    setting, 66-67
Maximize button, 9
menu bar, 6-7
Minimize button, 9
modes, 15-16
modifying templates, 99
mouse
    documents, 26-27
    menus, 6-7
    text, 27-28
moving text, 28-29

N–O

navigating documents, 26
Normal View, 20-21
numbering pages (documents), 71

opening
    documents, 25-26
    menus, 6-7
option buttons, 8
Options (Tools menu), 70, 85
Options command button, 18
Overtype mode, 15-16

P

page breaks, 69
Page Layout View, 21
Page Setup, 68
pagination, 63
    controlling, 67
    hard page breaks, 69-70
    numbering pages, 71

repaginating, 70
soft page breaks, 63
paper, 68
paragraphs, 54
aligning, 62
default settings, 65
finding marks, 38
formatting, 55-57
hanging indents, 60
indenting, 60-61
left indent setting, 61
tabs, 57-60
vertical alignment, 73-74
pasting text, 31-32
point sizes, fonts, 47-51
points, 49
portrait orientation (paper), 68
previewing documents, 67
printer fonts, 48
printing
documents, 23-24, 67, 85-86
Find File command method, 87
styles, 93
pull-down list boxes, 8

R

reducing views, 22
relating templates to documents,
96-98
removing section breaks, 72-73
renaming styles, 93
repaginating documents, 70
replacing text, 35-39
retrieving documents, 25-26
Ribbon
applying styles, 89
character formatting, 47
right-aligning text, 62
ruler, 55

S

saving documents, 17-20
screen fonts, 48
scroll bars, 26
Search button, 10
searching files, 83-84
section breaks
formatting, 73
removing, 72-73
vertical alignment, 73-74
selecting
templates, 98
text, 27-28
setting
margins, 66-67
paper orientation, 68
paper size, 68
small caps style, 51
soft page breaks, 63
sorting files, 82
special characters
finding/replacing, 35-39
inserting, 52-53
Special Spike Rule, 30
Spelling Checker, 40-41
spiking text, 29-31
split box, 5
status bar, 4
strikethrough style, 51
styles
character, 47, 51-52
documents
applying, 89
creating, 90-91
defining, 90
deleting, 92
printing, 93
renaming, 93
standard styles, 88-89
templates, 94
verifying, 92
viewing, 89

summary information (documents), 79-81
switching templates, 98
symbols insertion, 52-53
synonyms, 39

T

tabs, 57-60
  default settings, 65
  finding marks, 38
templates, 13
  boilerplate text, 99
  converting, 100-101
  copying, 98
  customizing, 101
  default, 98
  modifying, 99
  NORMAL.DOT, 13
  relating to documents, 96-98
  selecting, 98
  style templates, 94
  switching, 98
text
  aligning, 61-62
  boilerplate text, 99
  bullets, 53
  character styles, 51-52
  copying between documents, 31-32
  deleting, 33
  entering, 14-17
  finding/replacing, 35-39
  fonts, 48-51
  formatting, 47-48
  hanging indents, 60
  indenting, 60-61
  moving, 28-29
  pasting between documents, 31-32
  restoring deleted, 33
  selecting, 27-28
  spiking, 29-31

text boxes, 8
tunnel-through command button, 8
typefaces, 65

U-V

underlined text, 38, 51
Undo, 33
updating summary information (documents), 80-81
verifying document styles, 92
vertical alignment, paragraph spacing, 73-74
viewing
  documents, 20-23
  styles, 89
views
  changing, 22-23
  enlarging, 22
  Normal, 20-21
  Page Layout, 21
  Print Preview, 21
  reducing, 22

W-Z

windows, 31
word wrap, 15
WYSIWYG (What You See Is What You Get), 48

Zoom, 22

Learning is Easy with Easy Books from Que!

Que's Easy Series offers a revolutionary concept in computer training. The friendly, 4-color interior, easy format, and simple explanations guarantee success for even the most intimidated computer user!

Easy WordPerfect 6
Version 6

$16.95 USA
1-56529-087-9, 256 pp., 8 x 10

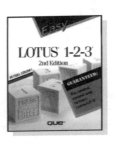

Improve with Hot Tips!

These unique guides teach readers shortcuts as well as powerful techniques—improving the proficiency of both novice and experienced users.